Adult Literacy Toolkit
Instructor Resources
English as an Additional Language Version

Adult Literacy Toolkit: Instructor Resources, English as an Additional Language Version
Copyright © Katharine Randell, 2017
First published 2017
Published by Adult Literacy Resources
Adelaide

Cover Design by Swamp Dragon Graficks

ISBN 978-0-6481653-0-9

Note on phonetic symbols used

The phonetic symbols used in the Macquarie Dictionary have been applied in this book. There are other phonetic systems that more closely represent Australian accents (such as the system developed by Harrington), but the Macquarie Dictionary has the advantage of familiarity for many instructors.

The symbols // are used to indicate sounds. The word 'chips' starts with the /ch/ sound.

Note on terminology

The term 'English as Second Language' (ESL), is used in many contexts. In this resource, the term English as an Additional Language or Dialect (EALD) is used because many learners speak multiple languages and are certainly not learning a 'second' language. Similarly, some learners speak a variant form of English that is substantially different from that spoken in urban Australia.

Contents

Figures and illustrations

Introduction

This resource was developed for instructors who are working with adults learning English as an additional language or dialect (EALD) and who had minimal or no formal education in their country of origin. Learning to read in an additional language as an adult poses some specific challenges and this resource was designed to address the needs of those learners. This book has been designed to be used by instructors working in a class environment, but it could be adapted to meet the needs of people who are tutoring individuals.

Method of development

This resource was developed to meet the needs of adult literacy learners who had minimal formal education in their country of origin, so the resources needed to be relevant to adults in Australia, and accessible to English language learners. The assumption in the development was that adult English language learners gain the language that is immediately relevant to them before gaining simpler, but less immediately relevant, vocabulary. It is entirely possible that an adult English language learner with diabetes will know the words *diabetes, monitor, glucose, sugar,* and other related words before they learn words like *pod* or *rim*, which are structurally simpler. This is not to suggest that adults can skip steps in learning to read and progress directly to complex authentic texts, but as much as possible, the words used in practice activities should relate to learners' existing vocabularies, interests, and experience.

The vocabulary bank was developed by extracting words on topics such as banking, government services, healthcare, housing, jobs, community services and local locations, and events. This built up a word-bank of about 25,000 words and phrases relating to life in Australia. This word bank was filtered to extract words with particular consonant-vowel patterns, or specific sounds and spelling patterns (see page 115).

No worksheets in this book

There are no worksheets in this book, unlike a book for children, simply because adults learning to read could be at vastly different stages of development for different skills. Learners may be reasonably proficient in letter formation and handwriting, or they may have never had the opportunity to develop those skills. Similarly, learners may have had minimal exposure to print before, they may use some decoding strategies, or they may have some unlearning of habits to do before making progress in reading. A series of worksheets simply won't meet the needs of classes with such a range of skill levels and experiences. The respective levels of skills could be significantly different depending on the learners in the class at the time as learners and demographics change. The aims of the class may also shift the focus; some classes with an employment focus may include writing, while people who are attending an evening class at a local community centre may have identified reading as a greater priority than writing. It is more appropriate for an instructor to choose targeted skill development exercises, such as phonemic awareness tasks, and handwriting and letter formation exercises, to suit the needs of learners, and to introduce letters and sounds at a pace that suits the class and scheduling. It is also possible that a class of adult learners, with multiple demands on time and attention, will need greater amounts of revision and review than a class learning to read in a primary school.

Approaches to Teaching Reading

The main methodology of language teaching in Australia is the communicative approach; the aim is for learners to develop communicative competence through using the language in meaningful ways. Learners complete roleplays, interviews, and gap fills, usually around a theme or topic. For example, learners could conduct a survey relating to the fruit preferences of people in the class and then participate in a role-play relating to buying fruit. In general, it is largely an effective approach to language teaching. While the communicative approach might be useful for developing language skills, and people have been successfully learning languages for thousands of years without sitting in classrooms, teaching people to read requires a different approach.

There have been changes in the approaches to teaching reading in recent decades. People have been quietly, and sometimes not so quietly, debating the best way to teach reading for a long time, but Whole Language grew out of Chomsky's ideas about language acquisition. The Whole Language approach to teaching reading was developed in the 1960s and it really took off in the decades after that. There are some complicated justifications, but at its most simple, Whole Language works on the idea that people are hard-wired to learn to speak a language through exposure, and children could learn to read the same way, through exposure rather than explicit instruction. Parents were encouraged to read to their children and were sometimes told they weren't reading enough if their children didn't make sufficient progress. In general, it's an inefficient approach to teaching reading skills, and the Australian government ceased funding the approach in 2005. Lots of children learnt to read in classrooms that used a Whole Language approach to teaching reading, but a certain percentage of children will learn to read despite the approach used by their teachers. It is certainly not the most effective or efficient teaching strategy, and it disproportionally disadvantages learners who are already at risk of not reaching their full potential; children from language backgrounds other than English, Aboriginal children, and children from low socioeconomic status backgrounds.

Debates about the relative merits of different approaches got very nasty (they were referred to as the 'Reading Wars') but apart from a few stragglers, early education in Australia has moved on. So now Australian primary schools are, generally, back to using phonics to teach reading. Whole Language has recently reappeared in slightly different form, as 'Balanced Literacy' but it is not the dominant approach to literacy instruction.

Phonics as a strategy for teaching reading has been around for a very long time. Teaching starts with sounds, and children are explicitly taught reading skills. In general, phonics is an effective and efficient approach to teaching reading skills.

The key concepts, commonly referred to as the 'Big Five', in literacy development are:

Phonemic Awareness: The understanding that spoken words are made up of sounds (phonemes), and the ability to hear and manipulate those sounds. Phonemic awareness is not an end goal, as much as a required skill that is essential for, and developed by, reading skills.

Alphabetic Principle, or phonics: An understanding of the link between printed letters and sounds, and the ability to use sounds to blend and read printed words. Systematic teaching of synthetic phonics is the most effective teaching strategy.

Fluency in reading: This requires automaticity in reading. The aim is that reading should become effortless and not require conscious attention. Fluency involves being able to read meaningful chunks of texts, not just words in isolation. This includes letter-sound correspondences, irregularly spelt words, and reading meaningful chunks of texts.

Vocabulary: The receptive and expressive use of vocabulary in meaningful ways. People learning English as well as learning to read may need to develop their vocabulary in order to be able to read.

Comprehension: The ability to extract meaning from texts.

All components are important, and the decoding of words is an important skill, but not enough for the reading of texts; comprehension strategies, knowledge of vocabulary and fluency in reading are also required. These skills need to be explicitly taught and developed with practice. These concepts are relevant for a child learning to read in the language that they have spoken all their life, and for adults learning to read for the first time in what may be their fifth language. Any literacy program should be evidence based, sequential and systematic. The ultimate aim is to help learners develop the skills to be independent readers who can go on to other education courses, work, or reach personal goals.

Key Point

- Reading involves a set of interrelated skills. It is not enough to simply decode words, there also needs to be an understanding of the sounds in words and the ability to read texts with comprehension.

The structure of written English

There are 42 to 44 phonemes (the smallest chunks of sound, such as /t/ or /ai/) in spoken English, with the exact number depending on the accent. These sounds are represented by 26 letters, which is obviously not a neat match, and some sounds are represented by two letters, such as the /sh/ in *shut*, and the /oa/ in *soap*. These two letters representing one sound are referred to as digraphs, and three letters representing one sound, such as *tch* or *igh*, are referred to as trigraphs. It is also possible to have spelling patterns, such as *ough* in the word *though*, which have four letters representing one sound in a word.

Digraphs are different from sound blends. Digraphs are written forms that represent one sound, such as *th* in *think*, or *sh* in *wash*; two letters are used to represent one sound. Blends are two or more sounds that are put together in words, such /fr/ in *frog*, or /nk/ in *pink*; both sounds are heard in the word. It is worth teaching learners to count the sounds in words very early in their literacy development, as this helps learners identify the difference between blends and digraphs.

The representation of sounds with 26 letters is further complicated by some letters and digraphs representing more than one sound, such as the *y* as in *yell*, *hungry* and *sky*, the *ow* as in *now* and *low*, or the *oo* in *foot* and *food*. There are also multiple ways to spell most sounds in English. For example, *boat*, *snow*, *mango*, *toe*, and *dough* all have the same sound in an Australian accent.

The most effective method of learning to read is a structured, systematic and sequential teaching program to help make sense of the multiple sounds that letters can represent, and the multiple representations of sounds that are used in English spelling. It is possible to point to spelling patterns that appear illogical, but around 80% English spelling does follow a logical pattern, even if it is a less common pattern. Yet more words have a logical pattern if the word origin is understood, and only about 4% of words are truly irregular.

It is worth making spelling patterns explicit to learners, simply because it is much more effective to teach a spelling pattern than to expect learners to memorise the spelling of hundreds of words.

Key Point

- It is more effective to teach spelling patterns than to expect learners to memorise unconnected and apparently illogically spelt words.

Learning vocabulary and learning to read

There is a difference between learning the English language and learning to read, and the two should not be conflated. An English language class might teach vocabulary according to different topics; clothes, festivals, food, shopping, health, and jobs are all frequent topics in English language classes. These are all potentially useful language topics and are important for vocabulary development, but may not be as useful for initial literacy activities.

In general, English language activities designed to develop knowledge of grammar or vocabulary should draw on the strengths of learners, such as speaking and listening, rather than expecting beginner learners to be able to read content. A vocabulary set related to a thematic topic, such as food, will contain a range of spelling patterns, some of which may be unfamiliar to learners, and so should be avoided as a reading exercise. However, it is possible to draw learners' attention to words that fit spelling patterns that have already been introduced to the class during the study of thematic topics, for example, words with the /ea/ sound, such as *meat, meal, treat, peanuts,* and *tea,* when learning food-related vocabulary.

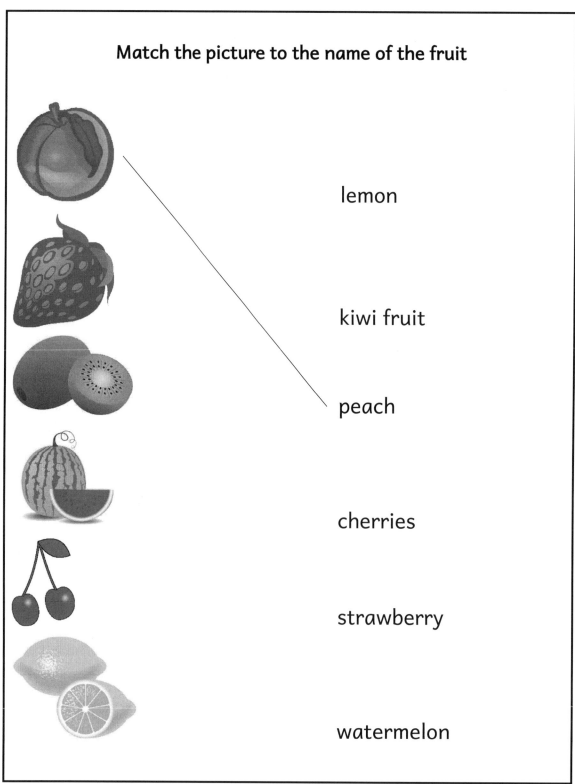

Figure 1: Matching exercise

There is an unspoken assumption built into the use of many English language exercises, such as matching tasks, that learners will acquire reading skills through exposure to texts (see Figure 1). This may be the case, at least to some extent, for people who have literacy skills in their languages of origin and are able to transfer those literacy strategies to reading English. However, that would not be the situation for someone who is learning to read for the first time in what might be their third language. People who are developing initial literacy skills often develop alternate strategies to complete a task, which may ultimately be counter-productive, such as looking at the first letter of a word and guessing. Tasks should be structured to meet the needs of learners, not hope that people will learn through exposure.

In a matching exercise with some fruit vocabulary, it may be possible to successfully complete the matching task using only the first letter of each word (see Figure 2). The learner feels a sense of satisfaction that they have completed the exercise, and their instructor thinks that their class is showing evidence of progress, but no reading has taken place, and the learner has potentially established that the best way to tackle reading exercises is to guess.

What the instructor intends learners to read	What the learners see
lemon	l□□□□
kiwi fruit	k□□□ f□□□□
peach	p□□□□
cherries	c□□□□□□□
strawberry	s□□□□□□□□□
watermelon	w□□□□□□□□□

Figure 2: What the learner sees

The vocabulary that a learner can successfully read will depend upon their current knowledge of sounds and their representation by letters.

Example

A hypothetical learner knows the sounds of the alphabet but does not know any digraphs or alternate spelling patterns. This means that they could read some words from a fruit vocabulary set, such as *fig* and *melon*, that they could decode with their current skill level, but they will need explicit instruction in decoding *grape* (which has a split digraph) and *peach* (which has the *ea* and *ch* digraphs).

Vocabulary	Aspect requiring attention or instruction		Vocabulary	Aspect requiring attention or instruction
apple	le		mango	o
apricot	a		melon	
banana	a		nectarine	i_e
blackberry	y		orange	ge
blackcurrant			pawpaw	aw
cherry	ch y		peach	ea ch
cranberry	y		persimmon	er
currant			pineapple	i_e le
fig			plum	
grape	a_e		pomelo	o
guava	u		raspberry	p y
kiwi	i		rockmelon	
lemon			strawberry	aw y
lime	i_e		tamarind	
lychee	y ch ee		tangerine	g er i_e
mandarin			watermelon	er

Figure 3: Fruit vocabulary set

10

In a fruit vocabulary set (see Figure 3), there are digraphs that need explicit instruction (*aw, ch, ea, ee, a_e, i_e, er*), alternate sounds for the spelling pattern (*ge, y*), vowels that need a little tweaking (*a, i, o*), one silent letter (*p*), and one less common spelling pattern (*u* giving the /w/ sound in *guava*). It is worth making the *le* pattern explicit, otherwise learners may expect that the sound is something like /leh/.

In the fruit vocabulary set, there are:

- o 9 words that are immediately decodable with a knowledge of the sounds of the alphabet.

- o 22 words that are decodable after explicit teaching of phonemes and spelling patterns.

- o 1 word that needs to be taught as an irregular spelling pattern because *u* giving a /w/ sound is a less common pattern.

This should not mean that vocabulary should not be taught, just there is a significant difference between teaching reading skills and teaching thematically-related vocabulary. Teaching the vocabulary and grammar structures of English should take into account the needs, abilities and interests of adults in the class, but it should not set learners up to fail by mixing vocabulary instruction with early literacy development.

It is important that exercises match the local pronunciation of words; it is frustrating for learners to complete an exercise and be told that their answer is incorrect because the pronunciation they have learnt is different from the one used in a worksheet. Answers should match the local pronunciation that students hear every day. For example, the final sound in the word *sister* could be /ər/, or it could be the unstressed sound /ɔ/ in an Australian accent. Similarly, a dictionary may indicate that the word 'library' has three syllables (li-brar-y), but if the local standard pronunciation is that the word has two syllables (li-bry), exercises should reflect that. If the aim is to teach a prestige form of English in the class, for example, specifically teaching learners use 'going to' rather than 'gonna', it may be worth choosing practice vocabulary where there is not a variance between the prestige variety of English and the common usage for early reading exercises. In the early stages of literacy development, it is worth using vocabulary that is highly familiar and reflects everyday usage.

Key Points

- There is a difference between teaching vocabulary and teaching reading skills. Conflating the two might have the unwanted outcome of effectively teaching learners to be instructor-dependent or to guess at words.

- The local accent and syllabification should be used when teaching literacy skills.

Teaching language

People have been successfully learning languages for far longer than people have been learning to read, and people in the class may be multilingual and already have highly developed language-learning skills.

Some general guidelines for teaching thematically-related vocabulary and grammar:

o Like any other language class, make sure there is a context for vocabulary development, as it is much easier to learn and retain vocabulary if there is a context for the language that is introduced, and ideally, a connection to existing knowledge.

o Use realia, visual images and role-plays to give context where possible.

o Specifically teach key words which adults need to be able to recognise in their daily life (*male, female, toilet, exit, doctor, chemist*) but otherwise avoid using written prompts for learnt vocabulary until learners can decode the words. Copying words that the learner cannot decode is not a good way to learn vocabulary or to learn to read.

o Rather than giving a written vocabulary list of thematically related words, such as a list of clothes, body parts, or food, teach the relevant vocabulary using images and realia, but only give the written words for items that learners can read. For example, learners might be able to read *belt, dress, handbag, hat, jacket, pants, pocket, socks, sundress* immediately and then *ring, stockings, singlet* when /ng/ is introduced, and *size, stripe* when /i_e/ is introduced. This is not to suggest that the same topic should be revisited after every sound and spelling pattern is introduced, but that the vocabulary can be given orally until learners can decode the relevant spelling patterns. Later, when a topic is revised, and more spelling patterns have been introduced, further written vocabulary can be given.

Difficult aspects of languages

Learning any language takes time and practice, no matter which language is being learnt. Some factors that influence the difficulty of learning a specific language are:

- How closely related a language is to another language (sometimes called 'linguistic distance'). Learning a closely related language is generally easier than a completely unrelated language. For example, Dutch is related to English, and so would generally be easier to learn for an English speaker than Thai, which is unrelated. Someone who has learnt Italian may find learning French easier because Italian and French are closely related and they may see the similarities.

- Similarities in the grammar. Mandarin and English, although they are unrelated languages, do have some similarities in grammar. In contrast, German, which is related to English, has some grammatical features that English has lost over time.

- Sounds that are in one language may not be present other languages, possibly making it difficult to pronounce words, or to differentiate between words.

- Language features such as tones, or if the language is syllable-timed or stress-timed.

- Factors relating to the individual person, such as the number of languages learnt previously, and the motivations for learning.

There are often newspaper and blog articles along the lines that English is the, or one of the, hardest languages to learn in the world. This might fill newspaper space, or feed the ego of people who speak English, but it is not necessarily true, and certainly not helpful to language learners if it discourages learning. Language learning can be very frustrating without being told that the language that they are struggling with is the most difficult in the world ('Is there any point in even trying if the language is that hard?'). Any language takes time and practice to learn, but it is not impossible. It is entirely possible that one of the most difficult aspects of learning English is speaking to monolingual English speakers, who because they are in a privileged position of speaking a language that is used in different contexts around the world, may have never been in the position of urgently needing to learn a language for daily tasks or employment.

It is not that English pronunciation is hard, or that English grammar is easy, so much as people will find certain aspects easier or harder depending on the languages that are already spoken. For example, a Mandarin speaker may find similarities in some grammar structures of English but struggle to identify or pronounce specific sounds. A computer programmer from a country with a lot of borrowed English vocabulary relating to technology may know a large body of nouns and verbs relating to their prior knowledge of computers but may struggle to form sentences.

For people learning to read in what may be their third or fourth language, there will be some aspects of reading in English that are more or less difficult, depending on their languages spoken. Learning to read involves more than simply decoding words, and learners' knowledge of the grammar, sounds, and vocabulary of the English language will have an impact on the process of learning to read. This is not to suggest that a person who speaks one language will find it easy to learn to read in English while another person who speaks a different language would find it difficult, but some features of languages will make certain aspects of learning to read in English more or less challenging.

Key Point

- The difficulty of learning to read in English will be influenced by a range of factors relating to the languages spoken by a learner.

Working with adults

Adults walking into a classroom will have the advantage of years of experience, and even learners who have never attended a class before may have very strong ideas about learning and the respective roles of the learner and instructor. These ideas may be worth explicitly addressing, particularly if the learner expectations do not match the philosophy of the class. Some learners may see the role of the teacher or instructor as that of a person who will impart information to receptive students, while the instructor may see their role as a facilitator in creating independent learners. Managing student expectations of their role and that of the instructor will go a long way towards avoiding learner frustration caused when, possibly unstated, expectations are not met.

- o Within the bounds of learners' language abilities, discuss the expectations of the class, the role of the learner and instructor, and why that teaching approach is taken. This can be something like, "I want you to learn to read anything. If you can only read words that I teach you, that does not help you on Saturday when you go shopping at the market, and I am not there."

- o During the process of learning to read and write, it can be useful to explain, within the bounds of learners' language abilities, why exercises are used so that learners can see a direct link between the exercise and the end goal. This can be as simple as saying something like, "Well done. That exercise is good for practising sounds. We need to use sounds for reading and writing."

Adults learning to read may have multiple demands on their time and attention, or they may believe that they are too old to learn. People may want to learn to read in an unrealistic time-frame so they can move on to further education or employment, and they may have the idea that 'children learn to read so it must be easy', which quickly turns to frustration when the process proves to be slower than anticipated. Some adults may find practice at home difficult due to family responsibilities, or shame at being less proficient at reading than their children. It is also possible that families will 'help' by performing reading homework on behalf of family members because task completion is perceived as being more important than the process of practice.

- o Help learners set achievable short-term goals with realistic timeframes. The goal 'learning to read' is too vague to be meaningful to learners as they progress and should be more specific. Goals will depend on the abilities and aims of learners, but could be to 'read four letter words', 'read *ea* and *sh* words', or to 'read the special words for the week'.

So far, the evidence is sparse, but it generally indicates that adults need the same sequence of stages as children learning to read; there are no easy short-cuts for adults wanting to learn to read quickly. Ultimately, the end goal is the same for both childhood and adult literacy instruction; to develop the skills of fluent, confident and independent readers. The aim is to explicitly teach skills so that learners can independently read outside the classroom, without requiring instruction in reading specific vocabulary. Any reading program that focuses on thematic vocabulary, rather than skill development, is likely to produce instructor-reliant learners, instead of independent readers. Although the sequences of skill development are similar for children and for adults, vocabulary, activities and pacing should be tailored to the needs of learners. It is not appropriate to use the same reading texts with adults as children, simply because the themes and vocabulary need to match the interests and needs of the learners.

- o Teach vocabulary and literacy skills separately. This will mean explicitly teaching thematic vocabulary (with possible mention of words that fit the theme and that have previously taught spelling patterns), and also explicitly teaching literacy skills (with possible reference to words that also fit with an ongoing class theme, such as clothing or food).

As well as interests and goals, adult classes will need to take into account:

- Existing phonemic awareness.
- Vocabulary and knowledge of English.
- Knowledge of phonics.
- Handwriting and letter formation.
- The attendance patterns of learners, and the need to revise certain skills.
- Computer literacy, as some learners may prefer to type, rather than learn to handwrite.
- Study skills, learning strategies and learners' experiences of education.
- Knowledge of Australian systems and structures.
- Motivations and expectations of learning in a class environment.

Key Points

- There is no quick short-cut for adults wanting to quickly learn to read.
- Exercises should target the needs and interests of people in the class as much as possible.

Making reading texts relevant

For adult English as an additional language or dialect (EALD) literacy learners, the language they need for daily life and participation in the community may far outstrip their ability to read that content. They may be able to negotiate the process of school enrolment for their children and talk about the relative merits of living in different suburbs, but any reading text is going to need to be far simpler. Giving learners reading texts that are above their current ability encourages people to guess the word based on the first letter, attempt some other ineffective strategy, or just give up.

Reading should be meaningful, not just a puzzle to solve, and discussion can add depth to reading materials. Learners may be able to decode simple sentences with consonant-vowel-consonant (CVC) words, such as *big* and *sit*, but in conversation, they may be capable of much more complex expression. "Sam had a bug." might be challenging to read, but conceptually, it can get fairly boring. Similarly, children's books about balls, puppies and football may be at the right reading level, but they may not be topics of interest in an adult migrant class. Ideally, a balance would be found between maintaining interest and developing reading skills. That meaning and interest can sometimes come from verbal extension questions and discussion. Conversations about pest eradication, rent, or anything else raised by the reading can add much more depth to exercises.

Strategies for making reading texts relevant to adult learners

- Choose appropriate vocabulary for the learners' interests as much as possible. The same sounds and spelling patterns need to be introduced in adult and children's classes, but there are choices that can be made about the vocabulary that is used to practice those sounds and patterns.
- Verbal extension questions and discussion.
- Use of visual imagery to extend the text.
- Drawing learners' attention to spelling patterns in other areas of the class.
- As much as possible, make reading a social activity. Team exercises and pair work can be more interesting and rewarding than plodding on individually.

Note on visual imagery: visual literacy is a learned skill just as much reading the printed word. It is worth making sure that images are understood by learners. It is also worth remembering that although visual images can add depth to a written text, a poorly laid-out text with multiple images can add to learners' cognitive load and make the successful reading of the text more difficult.

Working with traumatised adults

Learners at any age should feel safe in the classroom, but this is even more important for learners who have experienced trauma in the past. Learners in the class could have experienced significant trauma at some stage in their life, and for some learners that could be directly linked to education. In some countries, people who were educated or held specific occupations have been targeted for violence. In some places, learners are punished for incorrect responses with physical punishment, which could include caning or less common punishments such as standing barefoot in the snow. Even if learners do not explicitly state that they have experienced trauma in the past, it is common in adult language and literacy classes to have learners who have experienced horrific events.

o Make sure that learners feel in control and safe in the classroom. This includes making sure expectations are explicitly stated for attendance and participation if they are required.

o Make sure all exercises are clearly modelled so that learners know what is expected of them.

o Give positive feedback for attempts or participation, and give constructive feedback about corrections so that learners are very clear about what they got right and what they still need to work on.

o Help learners set reasonable expectations about progress and learning. This includes the speed that they can expect to learn to read and the level of proficiency attained. For example, some learners may have considerable difficulty pronouncing certain sounds that are not in their languages of origin; they may continue to have difficulty pronouncing the /sh/ sound, but they may learn to differentiate between /s/ and /sh/ and identify different words with those sounds.

o Learning does not have to occur in a classroom with all the desks facing the whiteboard. That layout may be comfortable for some instructors, but it is certainly not necessary for learning. Learners can develop literacy skills using a stick in the sand, a marker on the side of the fridge or with a laptop if that is the environment in which they are most comfortable. People were learning to read for a long time before there were whiteboards, and they will keep on learning as cultures and technology change. Alternatively, some learners may be most comfortable in an environment where the room is arranged according to their expectations of a classroom, with the instructor at the front and learners in rows.

o Do not imply that learners are, or should be, happy simply because they are in Australia. Some learners may have made a deliberate choice to move to Australia, others may have had that choice made for them due to conflict or a natural disaster. There may be complex feelings of guilt that they survived when other members of their family did not, feeling a loss of status if they have lost a specific role within their family or community, frustration at living within a new culture where they are a minority or anxiety for their children in an alien environment.

o Set learners up to succeed. In a literacy classroom, that means not giving learners work for which they are not yet ready, and acknowledging progress and successes as they occur.

- Have a clear classroom routine. This will entirely depend on your class, but a routine can help learners feel secure because they will know what to expect.
- Ensure there is continuity and consistency between instructors.
- Recognise that not every person will show emotion in the same way; some learners may become withdrawn rather than demonstrate distress or frustration.
- Recognise that learners will have good days and bad days.

Working with beginners

For learners who are just starting to develop their literacy skills, who may have had minimal exposure to written language, there are some additional factors to consider.

- Learners need to be explicitly taught that English is read from left to right at both a word and sentence level. For some learners, at least initially, it can be useful to move their left hand when starting to read a word or sentence, and then their right when they have finished the word or sentence.
- Fonts and handwriting on a whiteboard need to be very clear. For example, confident and skilled readers will be able identify that a a ɑ a ɑ a a a a are all the same letter (and are different from d ∂ d d d d d d ∂, q q q q q q q q q, and o o 0 o σ o o o o), but in the initial stages letters should be clear, consistent and easily identifiable. An analogy would be the difficulty reading a cursive Chinese character for 'water', 水, compared with a clear font, 水, for a Chinese language learner.
- Teach a correct pencil grip, which avoids muscle fatigue, from the initial stages of writing.

o Avoid introducing the letters **b d** or **p q** at the same time. These letters are easily confused, and learners may require relevant visual images to be drawn with the letters to help them learn the respective shapes of letters. A bat and ball image may not be appropriate for learners who have never had the opportunity to play organised sport, and so the phrase 'first the bat and then the ball' may not be a meaningful memory strategy, but another, more relevant, mnemonic could be used.

o Teach interim strategies. Ideally, learners will eventually be able to read and write a range of texts, but until those skills have been developed, it is useful for learners to know where they can access the spelling of personal details such as their full name, address, and other high-frequency data for forms.

o Some learners may have spent years working or raising children before attending English language or literacy classes and may never have spent extended periods sitting at a desk or may have developed back injuries at work. It may be worth structuring class activities so that there is some movement within the class rather than an extended time behind a desk. It is also worth encouraging learners to stand and stretch when they need to move.

o Even learners who are just beginning to develop literacy skills may have gained understandings of print and how to read which may or may not be accurate for reading English. This can include the formatting of dates, the sequencing of names, or the sounds linked to specific letters. These details can appear trivial until the implications are considered; writing a child's date of birth, the 8th of November 2003, as 03/11/08 could potentially have profound implications. This may need to be tactfully but explicitly corrected fairly quickly.

Terminology: talking with learners

It is important to keep terminology consistent within the class and between classes if learners move on as skills develop. Some terminology can be determined by the instructor; irregularly spelt words can be referred to as *irregular words*, *special words*, or even *green words*, if that suits the class. The concept of irregularly spelt words is unlikely to be found outside a classroom or educational context. As long as the term is consistent while the learners are developing reading and spelling skills, there is some scope for flexibility in naming the concept. It is worth avoiding the term 'difficult words'; these words might need more attention than other words, but they are still manageable.

Split digraphs, such as the *a_e* in *cake*, also require a term of reference that suits the class. The term *Magic E* would be far less appropriate in a multicultural adult class than in a primary school, although *Strong E* might suit a class. The term *Silent E* is best avoided, simply because the unintended message is that the letter is silent and so it can be safely ignored.

Some terminology is used outside the classroom and should be consistent with wider usage, such as *capital letters* and *lower case letters*. It is also important to avoid the terms *big letters* and *small letters* because some learners will simply write lower case letters at a larger scale (see Figure 4).

My name is Gul. compared with **My name is Gul.**

Figure 4: Big letters and capitals

There is not a correlation between *short vowels*, *long vowels*, and the length of sound articulation. The terms originate from the time in the eighteenth century when grammarians were drawing on Latin for guidance, ignoring the fact that Latin and English are different languages with dissimilar structures, and a grammar rule that was applicable to Latin is not necessarily applicable to English. In most Australian accents there are around twenty vowel sounds, not just five long and five short vowels. It is more helpful to explicitly teach specific sounds and spelling patterns than to introduce unhelpful terms.

| Terminology: talking with learners ||
Suggestion	Avoid
special words, or other terms that suit the class	difficult words
strong E	magic E, silent E
capital letters, lower case letters	big letters, small letters
specific sounds; the e sound, the ai sound	long vowels, short vowels

Figure 5: Terminology

Key Point

- Keep the terminology consistent within and between classes as much as possible.

Introducing the concept of letter sounds

In an adult class there may be any combination of people who have learnt the names of letters, those who can rattle off the alphabet song without connecting the names to the written letters, or learners who know a mix of letter names and sounds. Ideally, learners would learn the sounds first, then the letter names, but this is frequently not the case in adult classes.

It is important that learners can quickly and easily give the sound of each letter in isolation so that they can then blend sounds into words. People who learn that the letter *r* on the flashcard means 'r r r' will try to use that skill they have been taught to sound out words by saying "r r r e e e d d d", not "r e d... red". In the same way, learners who are taught that the flashcard shows 'b for ball' will try to decode words by saying "b-for-ball, e-for-elephant, d-for-door", which is not effective.

The first step in teaching sounds is to establish that there are letter names and letter sounds, and that they have different purposes. Learners need to understand that learning the letter sounds is directly relevant to reading; the letter names might be used when spelling out proper nouns on the phone, while sounds are used for reading and spelling.

Steps for introducing sounds

o Establish what learners know already. Some learners will have no knowledge of sounds and will give the letter names, while some learners may know a mix of sounds and names.

o Introduce or review the letter sounds: write the letters of the alphabet on the whiteboard. Give the sounds and ask learners to repeat.

o Illustrate why sounds, rather than letter names, are needed using highly familiar, easily decodable vocabulary.

Elicit the target vocabulary using pictures and realia. At this stage it is important that the vocabulary is highly familiar to the learners, such as *hat, leg, red, bag.*

Instructor: "Lee has new shoes. What colour are Lee's shoes?"
Learner: "Red."
(Write *red* on the board)
Instructor: "This is how we write red." (Pointing to the word)
Instructor: "Are-ee-dee." (pointing to the letters) "Lee has are-ee-dee shoes? Is that right?"
Learner: "No, red."
Instructor: "Good. Red. r-e-d red. We need the sounds."

Instructor: "What is this?" (point to your leg).
Learner: "Leg."
Instructor: "What are the sounds?" (point to the word on the board).
Learner: "El ee gee."
Instructor: "El-ee-gee? This is my eleegee. Is that right?" (point to your leg).
Learner: "No. Leg."
Instructor: "Yes, that's right. Leg. The sounds are l e g" (pointing to the letters on the board). "Leg. This is my leg. We need to use the sounds if we are reading."

o Review the sounds of the alphabet as a class.

o Introduce the actions if you are using the movements associated with specific sounds (see Figure 6). This is recommended but not essential and the choice will depend on the needs of the class.

o Review the letter sounds in random order, with learners working together in pairs.

o Learners practice reading CVC words in pairs. It is important that letter sounds are closely linked to reading. Letter sounds should be immediately used to read familiar words, rather than just being random symbols to memorise.

Make it clear to people that learning the sounds of the alphabet is just the first stage of learning to read. If learners treat the alphabet as the only reading tools they need, digraphs and alternate spellings will be ignored or become very frustrating. Even if this is not intended, having the alphabet but not digraphs on the wall of the classroom can give the impression that the alphabet is the only tool that is needed for reading. Rather than decorating the room with the A-Z letters, it may be more useful to display recently studied or reviewed digraphs if language content is displayed.

The sounds that are challenging for specific learners may depend, at least in part, on their languages of origin, and it may be worth drawing learners' attention to specific sounds that are being produced inaccurately. It may be necessary to make it clear to learners that some sounds are quieter than others (/f/ /h/), some sounds can be drawn out without changing the sound (such as /s/ /m/) and others can't be extended without changing the sound (such as /p/ /b/). Attempting to make /h/ louder, or /p/ longer, gives an incorrect sound.

Instructor: (miming thinking, then writing *hat* on the board) "huh! a t…" (pointing to the letters) "huh!-at. Raoul has a green huh!-at today. Is that right?

Learner: "No. Hat. He has a green hat."

Instructor: "Good. It is a hat. h a t" (pointing to the letters) "The h sound is quiet. It is not huh!"

It is worth making it clear to learners that /x/ is made up of two sounds /ks/. This is a difficult sound for some learners because the word they most frequently encounter that has the letter *x* at the start is *x-ray*, which uses the letter name rather than the sound. It is more difficult to identify sounds at the end of words than at the start so the /ks/ sound at the end of common words like *box* and *six* may not be easy to identify. Similarly, the /ng/ sound, such as in the word *long*, can be difficult to identify for related reasons, as it is not found at the start of words in English.

Key Points

- It is important that learners clearly understand the difference between letter sounds and letter names.

- Specific sounds may need more attention than others, depending on the languages that learners speak.

Blending

Blending is the process of putting sounds together to make a word, and it is a skill that learners need to be explicitly taught. This means showing them how to identify the sounds in words and to connect them together. There are hundreds of potential letter blends, and around fifty initial and final blends that are commonly found in English, such as *bl* and *dr*, and so it is much more effective to teach learners how to blend sounds, rather than to recognise specific letter blends.

Oral blending

Make sure that learners have had plenty of exposure to oral blending of sounds before they start to blend letters on a page. Instructors can model blending one and two syllable words before learners start attempting to read. This can be given as a spoken demonstration, as in, "s i t   sit. l o s t   lost", before learners attempt to blend sounds into words themselves. The aim is to help learners hear that the words are made up of individual sounds and to understand that they can put those sounds together.

In the initial stages of people learning to read, it is important that the words that are sounded out by an instructor are highly familiar to learners. A learner who can connect the sounds /p l u g/ with the word *plug* is likely to have a lot more difficulty hearing the word *glum* due to a lack of familiarity. Unfamiliar words can be used later, but in the initial stages, words should be part of learners' everyday vocabularies.

When learners can hear the word if it is sounded out, they can move on to sounding out a written word themselves. Make sure that learners attempt to read the word that is in front of them, not simply look at the first letters of words and guess. A learner who is presented with the word *swim* and responds "swimming pool" is using skills that may help them function in the community with minimal literacy skills, but it is not reading the word that is in front of them.

Make sure that learners are saying the sounds as correctly as possible. There is probably going to be transference from their languages of origin for learners who speak languages other than English, but as much as possible they should attempt an accurate use of sounds. For example, this means teaching learners to use the sound /d/ without adding 'uh'; the sound is /d/ not /duh/, or /l/ not /luh/. It is much harder to hear the word *big* in /buh-i-guh/ than /b i g/. For similar reasons it is important to teach sounds not phrases, for example, /z/ not 'z, zoo' or 'z for zoo'. Learners need to be able to use and manipulate sounds, and teaching 'z for zoo' means that some learners will rattle off, "z-for-zoo i-for-insect p-for-pen" and so will be unable to sound out /z i p/.

Make sure that learners can give the sounds automatically. If the sounds are drawn-out because learners are struggling to remember the sound, it is harder to blend the sounds to make a word. 'h........a........t' is much harder to blend than 'h a t'. This can take a lot of short periods of practice over time. This practice should be concurrent with reading practice because memorising sets of letters and sounds will be much less effective if it is not directly connected to reading.

Once learners are confident with decoding and blending sounds, introduce the process of tweaking sounds. Some words have small variations in the sound and spelling patterns and would not be considered an irregular spelling pattern, but they do require alternate sounds. For example, *pasta* in an Australian accent is likely to be pronounced /pɑstə/. Teach learners to try alternate vowel sounds if what they are reading is not making sense, but this does require that the vocabulary is highly familiar.

Key points

- Teach learners how to blend, rather than teaching specific blends.

- Allowing for transference from other languages, help learners to differentiate between sounds and to produce sounds as accurately as possible.

Non-words

Non-words have a role in the literacy development of children in schools as they can be useful practice and they can be a good check of decoding skills. Children may have memorised frequently used words in readers or spelling lists but would not have memorised a set of non-words, which makes them a good check for decoding skills; if learners can decode words like 'flib' or 'poat', it indicates that they have mastered the decoding of the relevant sounds.

Non-words should have less of a role in the literacy development of adults who speak English as an additional language. The process of learning to read in another language is slow and frustrating without introducing meaningless words into the classroom. If an indication of decoding skills is required, it may be more appropriate to use words outside the learners' current vocabulary or less frequently used English words. Any word not in a learner's current vocabulary, such as *coop* or *glide*, could be used instead of non-words, but it is still suggested that the words are explained after the reading task has been completed.

Making learning multisensory

Current evidence suggests that one of the best strategies for children to learn to read and to spell is to make exercises multisensory. There is far less evidence in relation to adult EALD learners than children, but so far, all indicators are that multisensory learning can support adult learners who are developing language and literacy skills.

It is possible to link an action to each sound that is taught, such as the action of unlocking a door being linked to an /u/ sound. It is entirely possible to teach reading and writing without using actions linked to sounds, the actions are simply one more tool to help learners, but for learners who already face difficulties in learning to read, it is worth considering any tools that are available.

Movements can reinforce sounds and help commit sounds to memory, but the movement should be relevant and appropriate for adult learners. Using movement also helps learners link alternative spellings; learners can see that the same movement is used for *ai, ay, a_e,* and *ei*.

If movements are going to be used by the class, it is worth teaching actions associated with the letters and sounds that are already known as well as those for new digraphs. Learners may be confident using the /l/ sound and the letter representation, but there are other spelling patterns such as *le,* and *ll*. Using the actions can help learners draw connections between different spellings and the same sound. Similarly, the /k/ sound may be spelt as *c, k* or *ck*, and it is useful to differentiate /k/ from /s/ in words like *city*.

The movements below are suggestions; there is no reason that alternate movements can't be substituted so this is a chance to make the movements meaningful to learners. Choosing actions that learners can identify with will help the movements be remembered (although this is going to be much easier with some sounds than others). If a learner regularly brings in food to share with the class, miming eating those banana cakes will be much more meaningful than an action without a connection to the class. It is important that movements are consistent between classes if learners move from one class to the next as their language skills develop. Another point to remember is that if alternate movements are chosen, make sure the sounds and action associated are not going to confuse learners, for example 'eating an egg' has both the /i/ and the /ɛ/ sounds and should be avoided because the sounds are too similar.

It is not appropriate to use the same sound-movement patterns with adult EALD learners as children's phonics programs; the /ie/ sound being associated with pirates can be entertaining for children who grew up watching funny pirates with silly hats on television in Australia, but for some adults, Somali or South East Asian pirates are a traumatic reality. Learners may be aware of jelly, for example, but if it is considered something that their children might have a friend's party and that they have never tried, jelly is not personally relevant to them and is unlikely to be a meaningful way to remember a sound. Similarly, puppies might be cute members of the family in some cultures, while for some learners dogs could be considered unclean or a pest with a real risk of rabies. It is also worth avoiding animal sounds as a link to phonemes because the representation of animal sounds is culturally determined; ducks may 'quack' in English, but they may say 'vak' in Turkish, or 'coin' in French.

The aim is to introduce sound and letter correspondences and then get learners reading, not to teach new vocabulary during reading development exercises, so only use vocabulary that learners can confidently use. People are learning how to graphically represent and so new vocabulary should be introduced at a different time. For that reason, it is important to target the narrative to the level and interests of learners in your class.

Process of introducing the sounds and movements

- Introduce a narrative: this can be short and should be something familiar or relatable for learners.

    /d/ "I like eating tomatoes. I want to grow some tomatoes in my backyard. I need to **dig** lots of holes in the ground for the seeds and the plants." (Mime digging holes in the ground).

- Demonstrate the sound and the action.

- Learners make the sound and the action.

- Show the letter on the board or a flashcard.

- Write some practice words on the whiteboard from the Word Bank. These should be words that learners know and are confident using, as the aim is decoding practice, not the introduction of vocabulary. Learners being able to say, "h-a-n-d… hand!" and wiggling their fingers to show comprehension is much more useful than, "d-a-n-k… dan… dank… Is dank a word?"

- Learners decode the words on the board.

- Discussion around the words. This is a chance to make the reading practice relevant for learners, it should not just be a random group of words with no connection beyond a spelling pattern; hopefully the words have some relevance to learners.

    Learner: "r…e…n…t… ren..t…. rent!"
    Instructor: "Do you pay rent?"
    Learner: "For my house."
    …

- Show how the letter is written on the board

- Show the letter formation in the air.

- Learners form the letter in the air.

- Copy some sample words from the board (for a class that is reasonably confident with letter formation). This is an opportunity to use a Wordbook.

  or

  Trace dotted letters, then the write letters on their own (for learners who are developing writing skills).

- If possible, a few further practice words are put on the board for reading and discussion.

- Remind learners that the important aspect to remember is the sound and how we write the sound, they don't have to go home and memorise the words which are just for reading practice. This is particularly important for learners who are in the habit of copying work from the board without comprehension because they associate learning with rote memorisation.

The use of the actions will depend on the aims, interests and demographics of the class. In some classes, the actions might be seen as a welcome chance to move.

Possible uses of the actions in the classroom:

- o Use the actions when new sounds and spelling patterns are introduced. This helps to draw connections between sounds as learners can see that *or, aw, au,* and *ore* have the same action.

- o Use the actions when learners are studying spelling words, which may help the retention of spelling patterns.

- o Pairs exercises, such as one learner performing the actions for a word and another learner identifying the actions and blending the sounds together to make the word.

Sounds and actions

Sound		Action
a	æ	Brush **ants** off your arm
b	b	Hand far apart to show something **big**
c, ck, k	k	Pretend to **cut** some paper.
d	d	**Dig** a hole in the ground
e	ɛ	Wave goodbye at the **end** of the day
f, ph	f	Move hands like a **fan**
g	g	**Give** another learner something
h	h	Breathe on your **hands** as if they are cold
i	ɪ	Pretend to get **ink** on your hands
j, g	dʒ	Pretend to put on a **jumper**
l	l	Point to your **lip**
m	m	Pretend to **mix** in a bowl
n	n	**Nod**
o	ɒ	Pretend to turn **on** the light
p	p	Pretend to **pick** apples
r	r	Pretend to **rip** some paper
s, c	s	Hold up **six** fingers
t	t	Pretend to turn on **tap** and wash hands
u	ʌ	Pretend to **unlock** a door
v	v	Pretend to chop **vegetables**
w	w	Move your arm like a tree in the **wind**
x	ks	Pretend to open a **box**
y	j	Put your hands near your mouth and pretend to **yell**
z	z	Pretend to open a **zip** on your jumper

Sound		Action
ai, a_e, ay	eɪ	Put two index fingers and two thumbs together to make a triangle
ar	a	Pretend to drive a **car**
ch	tʃ	Pretend to **chop** vegetables
ee, e_e, ea, y	i	One hand shading your eyes, pretend to **see** something
er	ɜ	Pretend to be thinking
ie, i_e, igh, y	aɪ	Point to your **eye**
ng	ŋ	Use your hand to show a **swing**
oa, o_e, ow	oʊ	Pretend to be surprised
oi, oy	ɔɪ	Pretend to be celebrating – Oi! Oi! Oi!
or , au, aw, al	ɔ	Point to two things – ___ **or** ___
ou, ow	aʊ	Rub your shoulder and say **ow!**
sh	ʃ	Put one finger in front of your mouth – **sh!**
ue	ju	Point to someone else (**you**)
qu	kw	Pretend to write **quickly**
oo	ʊ	Point to your **foot**
oo ue	u	Pretend that you have **glue** on your fingers
th th	θ ð	Hold up right hand and raise one finger for each sound

Figure 6: Sounds and actions

This is not intended as a complete list of alternate spellings of sounds as there are further spellings of some sounds.

Making spelling multisensory

It is useful to make a spelling program multisensory for the same reason that a phonics program could be multisensory; it is one more tool for helping students develop and retain skills. Making spelling practice multisensory does not replace explicit instruction, but it can help learners remember spelling patterns and irregularly spelt words. As with any exercise, strategies need to be adapted to the needs and interests of learners. Some strategies require movement and can be useful for a class that has been sitting for a period of time.

Ways of making spelling and writing multisensory

- Write the word on an alternate surface (on a whiteboard, in steam on a mirror, with water on a wall, in sand with a stick, or in salt on a baking tray).

- Write the word in the air with a hand, making the letters as large as possible.

- Write the word in the air with a foot (while sitting down).

- Learners in pairs spell out words aloud, throwing a tennis ball or beanbag between the pair each time a sound is given.

- Type the words on a computer.

- Spell out the word: consonants said softly and vowels said loudly. Note: for EALD learners, vowels are often far harder to differentiate and manipulate than consonants. Saying the vowels more quietly and the consonants more loudly can make the task much more difficult.

- Learners work in pairs, one person silently spells out spelling words, the other person attempts to lip-read. There may be a low level of accuracy or success on the part of the lip-reading partner, but for some classes it can be a fun exercise. This may need to be mentioned before the exercise so that learners do not find the task simply frustrating.

Materials and resources

There is a massive industry supplying resources for children developing literacy skills. These resources vary widely in quality, but there is a wide range of options for people teaching children to read. It is possible to spend a small fortune on wall posters, flashcards, and online game access, which might help learners, but in general, are not essential. There are far fewer resources for adults learning to read, and so greater creativity on the part of instructors is needed.

Essential resources for classroom teaching

- Something for the instructor to write on: whiteboard, smartboard, blackboard, or large paper pad

- Markers

- Learner notebooks

- Pens or pencils for learners

> or

- Laminated lined pages and fine-point whiteboard markers for learners

- Instructor resources; word lists for exercises, and exercises,

- Flash cards: A4 paper with single letters and digraphs printed.

- Practice materials at an appropriate level

Tip: If you are making your own flash cards, put a small mark or line indicating the top or bottom of every page; it is very easy to end up with the sheets with d/p, b/q and u/n transposed. Do not only mark specific pages because people learn to use additional marks, even thumbprints, as indicators.

For learners who have had traumatic experiences in the classroom, or feel that learning to read is something that children do, it is entirely possible to teach reading with whatever resources come to hand, such as using markers on the side of a fridge, if that is where they feel most comfortable. Learning to read does not only happen in classrooms with learners facing a whiteboard.

Some learners are reluctant to show a lack of proficiency in writing and are unwilling to write in notebooks, which will show their, perceived, lack of ability. For these learners, a laminated lined page may enable them to gain writing practice without committing to the permanency of writing in a notebook. The writing task can be wiped as soon as it has been completed and feedback has been given. The aim is to help learners develop reading skills and if writing on a wipeable surface facilitates that, then it may be a useful strategy. More advanced learning strategies, such as learner-developed word-lists and on-going records of learning, can be established later, once more confidence in reading has been developed.

Optional resources

These are not essential but are a very good idea, if they are available:

- A wordbook for learners to complete.

- Printed resources that learners can take home for practice.

- A smartboard, or computer and data projector. These make it much easier to show images as topics are raised in class.

- Sound card sets for each learner to use and manipulate during exercises.

- A set of picture cards for use in phonemic awareness exercises.

A set of sound cards should have one letter or digraph printed on each card and be large enough for learners to easily manipulate (see Figure 7). They are useful for exercises that require learners to manipulate sounds as they give people something to physically move. Sound cards can be made with cardboard or plastic bottle-tops, but paper tends to be too flimsy to survive more than one exercise. It is worth making sets of sound cards that will last; a complete set of sound cards for each learner involves a lot of cutting-out and doing that each time there is a phonemic awareness task is not practical. Making sets of laminated or cardboard sound cards saves a lot of time in the long term.

Sound card

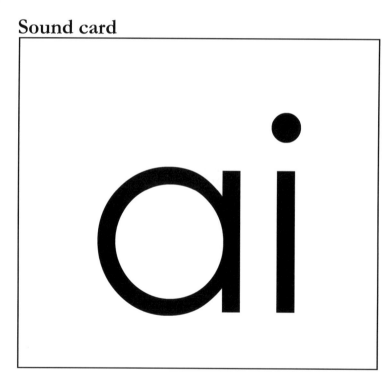

Figure 7: Sound card

Sample from a learner Wordbook

__bike_____   __mine_____

__ride_____   __time_____

i_e __side_____   __outside_____

__nine_____   _____

__ripe_____   _____

__bite_____   _____

__soap_____   __cockroach_____

__road_____   _____

oa __coat_____   _____

__toast_____   _____

__oats_____   _____

__throat_____   _____

Figure 8: Sample from a wordbook

Wordbooks can be useful for learners to develop over time. As each digraph is introduced, example words can be written by learners in the spaces (see Figure 8). It is important to stress to learners that this is not a complete list of words with this spelling pattern and that the words are simply some examples. This can be further reinforced by adding to the word bank over time as vocabularies develop. As more digraphs are learnt, previously completed sections of the word bank can be revised, for example, later adding the word *outside* to the *i_e* section when the *ou* digraph has been studied or adding *throat* and *cockroach* to the *oa* section once *th* and *ch* have been studied. It is also important to reiterate to learners that the digraph is the part to memorise, not the sample words. For learners who have an expectation that learning requires rote memorisation, it may be useful to direct their attention to digraphs, rather than word lists of thematically unconnected words.

Online visual dictionaries, which have sound recordings of thematically grouped vocabulary words, can be very useful for EALD literacy learners, but standard dictionaries, and even learner dictionaries, require relatively advanced literacy skills and so are of less use to EALD literacy learners.

Making text visually accessible

A certain percentage of the population has barriers to reading such as dyslexia. The exact numbers vary according to the study, but approximately 7% of the population is affected by dyslexia to some degree, meaning that in a class of 20 EALD literacy learners it is safe to assume that one or two people will have additional barriers to learning to read which will almost certainly be unrecognised. For adult EALD learners who are developing literacy skills in what may be their third or fifth language, it is extremely difficult to differentiate between the difficulties caused by dyslexia and the difficulty of learning to read in another language. It is not the role of a language or literacy instructor to label or diagnose learners with reading difficulties; that is the role of an educational psychologist, and it takes a battery of tests to get an accurate profile of a learner. However, strategies to meet the needs of learners with dyslexia do not disadvantage other learners in the class, and can generally be considered good teaching practices.

o Keep fonts clear. Generally, a clear, san serif font such as **Arial**, **Verdana**, **Tahoma**, or **Trebuchet** is recommended. **Comic Sans** and **Century Gothic** have the additional advantage of having a and g letters that most closely resemble a handwritten shape (**ag ag**). There are other fonts available for download online, but the fonts listed are generally available as standard in MS Office packages. Fonts that have been specifically designed for readers with dyslexia have had very mixed reviews so far.

o 12-14 point font size can be a useful start, although it is common in adult classes to have learners who need a larger font size due to deteriorating eyesight.

o Allow plenty of spacing on printed pages; 1.5 line spacing, and spaces between paragraphs.

o Avoid using red and green markers on a whiteboard. These can be hard to read on reflective surfaces and hard to differentiate for people who are colour-blind.

o Avoid long strings of text written continuously on the whiteboard. 60-70 characters is a useful guideline.

o Keep the space around the whiteboard clear and uncluttered. It can be tempting to decorate around the whiteboard with visual prompts of grammar, irregularly spelt words, and the alphabet or digraphs, but this can add to learners' cognitive load. Putting decorations and prompts elsewhere in the classroom, away from the whiteboard, might be more appropriate.

o Make sure that letters are clearly distinguishable on a white board and in printed material. Learners reading or copying words such as *camot* instead of *carrot*, or *doud* instead of *cloud* may be an indication that they cannot perceive individual letters clearly.

Rather than there being a single ideal font for an EALD class, there will probably be a range of fonts that are used over time (see Figure 9). Comic Sans and Century Gothic may be the most useful for learners when they are starting to read individual words and phrases, because of the letter a and g shapes, but Century Gothic may be less useful for reading sentences and longer texts because the capital I is too easily confused with a lower case letter l. It is more difficult for learners to read fonts that do not clearly differentiate between a capital I, a lower case l, or a number 1 (see Figure 10). A fluent reader who is also confident using English may be able to read a text with little difficulty, and may not even notice that some different letters appear to be the same shape because they know what to expect in a given word or phrase. For learners who are developing literacy skills, English language skills, or both, it is important that the letters are obviously different.

	Lower case a	Lower case g	Capital I	Lower case l	Number 1
Arial	a	g	I	l	1
Verdana	a	g	I	l	1
Tahoma	a	g	I	l	1
Trebuchet	a	g	I	l	1
Comic Sans	a	g	I	l	1
Century Gothic	a	g	I	l	1

Figure 9: Fonts

I flew from Ireland to Iceland late last night.   (Arial)

I flew from Ireland to Iceland late last night.   (Comic Sans)

Figure 10: Capital I and lower case l distinction

Pacing and sequencing of sounds

Sounds should be introduced quickly enough that learners maintain interest but not so fast that they cannot retain and integrate the new skills. In practice, this means that different classes will have altered pacing; a class that meets for five hours a day, three times a week, will have a very different pacing from a class that meets for two hours a week. It is also common for adult learners to have competing demands for their time and attention, which can lead to erratic attendance patterns and a greater need for revision and review.

Avoid introducing alternate spellings of the same sound until learners are confident decoding that spelling pattern. For example, *ai* could be followed by introducing *sh*. Introducing all /ai/ spelling patterns at once involves giving learners sets of words like *rain, made, day, vein, they, break, basic, eight*. Presenting learners with patterns such as *ai, a_e, ay, ei, ey, ea, a, eigh* all at once simply leaves learners with the idea that English spelling is an impenetrable mess. Ideally, one spelling of the /ai/ sound is introduced at a time, and learners become confident using that representation of the sound before others are introduced. A worksheet with a range of alternate spellings of the same sound may be a useful review for learners, but it is not a good way to introduce sounds and alternate spellings.

For learners who start the class with a half-understood command of the letter names, or the ability to rattle off the alphabet song, the first step is to shift the focus from letter names to letter sounds (see Figure 11).

Prior knowledge and teaching sequence

Learners' prior knowledge	Learners know no letter names or sounds	Learners know some sounds and letter names, but use them inter-changeably	Learners know the letter names but not sounds	Learners know the letter names and sounds of the alphabet	Learners know some of the letter names and sounds of the alphabet, and some digraphs
Teaching sequence	Gradually introduce letters and sounds. When learners are confident decoding words and blending sounds, then move on to digraphs.	Introduce the concepts of letter names and sounds, and the contexts in which they are applied. Make sure that learners are confident using sounds to decode words and blending, and then move on to introducing digraphs and alternate spellings.		Revise the letter sounds. Review blending and sounding out. Gradually introduce digraphs and alternate spellings.	Revise the letter sounds, with emphasis on sounds that are missing or forgotten. Review blending and sounding out. Fairly quickly introduce digraphs and alternate spellings.

Figure 11: Prior knowledge

Changing habits

Some learners will walk into the classroom being able to rattle off the alphabet song but unable to match letters to the letter names, while others may be able to match letter names to the written forms. In some regards, learners who can do neither may have the advantage because they don't need to change reading habits in order to be able to learn to read.

In an adult learning setting, some learners will need to unlearn habits before they can learn new skills. These could have been survival skills in the early stages of their language development, such as looking at the first letter and guessing the word, but ultimately this can be unhelpful. It might be necessary to draw learners' attention to ineffective strategies as well as teaching new skills.

The first step is to introduce the idea that letters have a sound and a name. For learners with a farming background it is possible to draw on prior knowledge:

> "This is a goat. It has a name, goat. It has a sound" (in some classes, learners will make goat sounds unprompted. Alternatively, show a YouTube clip of goats bleating). "Does a goat say, *Goat, goat, goat?*" (No) "Good. Letters are the same. Letters have a name and a sound. We need the sounds for reading."

Rolling intake

Ideally, early literacy skills would be introduced in an appropriate, cumulative sequence, but this is generally not possible in adult classes. One of the biggest differences between teaching children to read in a school and teaching adults in English or literacy classes is attendance.

Whether or not it is the case, schools are generally designed for children to start school with the same age group, who are assumed to be at roughly the same stage of development, and then, sickness aside, to attend school regularly. In contrast, adult classes often have a rolling intake of learners, and once learners have started classes, they may have different scheduled attendance patterns and erratic attendance due work and family commitments.

For advanced English language learners, a rolling intake may be a challenge but manageable. A learner might start a class in the middle of one topic but then be able to competently complete the next unit undertaken by a class. For learners who are just starting their literacy studies, a rolling intake and erratic attendance can complicate the process of learning to read.

Key features of well-designed literacy programs for children are that they are sequential and cumulative. For example, students would be introduced to the sound /sh/ and may learn to read words like _ship_ and _shop_. Later on, learners would be introduced to the sound /oo/ and only then would they start reading words like _shampoo_ and _mushroom_. For adult classes, this sequential, cumulative development of skills would be ideal but is generally not realistic. For this reason, the materials used in this book have been designed to be used in stages rather than being cumulative.

Strategies for managing a rolling intake

   o High frequency of revision. This enables continuing learners to consolidate skills and new learners to be introduced to sounds and concepts.

   o Small groups working at different stages, possibly merging into larger groups as appropriate.

   o Peer teaching with highly confident learners.

Stages

The resources in this book have been developed to be used in three stages; the sounds of the alphabet, digraphs, and alternate spellings.

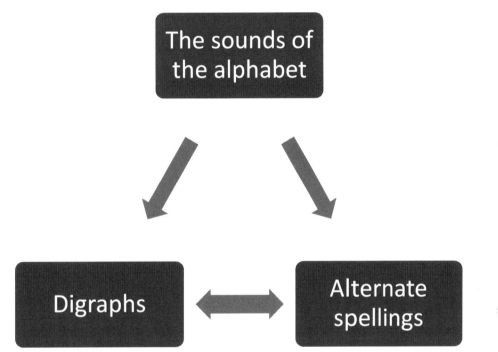

Figure 12: Stages

The aim is that once learners are confident in using the sounds of the alphabet, it possible to continue from any point in the introduction of digraphs or alternate spellings. For example, it is entirely possible that a learner starts mid-semester, learns the sounds of the alphabet and then continues with the rest of the class in studying alternate spellings. Each introduction of a sound or spelling pattern has been designed to be self-contained. This omits the cumulative practice of words like *shadow* because it contains both *sh* and *ow*, but enables learners to start at any point once they have learnt the sounds of the alphabet. Because learners could potentially start at any time in a class with a rolling intake, it is important to track the starting point and progress of learners. Although it is possible to have learners starting at different points, all learners still need to cover the same material; the only difference should be the order in which sounds and spelling patterns are studied, not the material covered.

It is important to mix the sounds when completing revision. It is much easier to practice a single sound at a time, such as *see, tree, bee* and *need.* Reading *rain, tree, tie, chip,* and *shut,* requires that learners identify a range of sounds in words. This is why accurate tracking of learner progress needs to be accessible and up to date; frequent review exercises should target the current needs of learners.

There are examples of tracking grids on Page 110 (See Figure 29). The aim is to record which spelling patterns have been introduced and reviewed by specific learners so that all sounds and spelling patterns are covered by each person in a program, even if learners start studying at different times.

It is not recommended to simply give learners workbooks to work through independently. Learning to read is going to be more effective and rewarding if it is a social activity; language and reading are for communication, not just puzzles to be decoded.

Key Points

- Learners can start at any point once they are confident using the sounds of the alphabet.

- Learners need to cover all the material, only the sequencing may vary. Instructors will need to track the progress of learners to make sure that sounds and spelling patterns are not omitted.

The sequence of sounds

There is currently no clear evidence that one sequence of sound introduction in a phonics teaching program is any more effective than any other, but some sequences have the advantage of allowing learners to start decoding words very quickly. Introducing 'a b c d e' does not allow many words to be formed and even fewer words that are familiar to EALD learners.

For learners who know some sounds, or know the letter names of the alphabet, it is useful to introduce the letter sounds fairly quickly.

Sequence of Sounds

	Letters and digraphs to introduce	Skills and concepts to introduce
Set One	Sounds of the alphabet: s a t i p n c k e h r m d g o u l f b j z w v y x	Double letters, for example ll, ff
		Simple blends
		Irregular spelling
		Capitals and lower case letters
		Counting sounds in words
Set Two	ch sh ai oa ie ee or ng oo th qu ou oi ue er ar	More complex blends
		More irregular spelling words
Set Three	a_e e_e i_e o_e u_e y /ee/ ay /ai/ oy /oi/ ea /ee/ y /ie/ ow /oa ou/ ir /er/ ew /ue oo/ ur /er/ igh /ie/ aw /or/ wh /w/ au /or/ ph /f/ al /or/	More complex blends
		More irregular spelling words

Figure 13: Sequence of sounds

<u>Set One</u> is made up of sounds of the alphabet without the letter q (see Figure 13). Q can be introduced with other digraphs in Set Two because in English the /kw/ sound is written *qu*, and *q* without the *u* is only found in names and words that have been borrowed from other languages, such as the word *Iraq*.

It is good to introduce the concept of blends and digraphs at this stage. Teach learners to count the sounds in words and make sure that learners are aware there may be a difference between the number of letters and the number of sounds in words before introducing digraphs. Teach learners to count the sounds in words, starting with simple words and highly familiar words with double letters, such as *bill, kiss* and *off*.

Teach learners how to blend rather than encouraging memorisation of specific blends. Once learners are confident using the sounds of the alphabet and blends, they can move on to learning the sounds in Set Two or Three.

<u>Set Two</u> introduces one written form of sounds. Similar to the introduction of alphabet sounds, there is not currently clear evidence that one sequence is more effective than another, but for adult EALD learners there are additional considerations. Sounds that are not present in learners' languages of origin will require additional practice. For example, many languages do not use /th/ sounds and so these may pose more of a challenge than sounds that are familiar. Similarly, differentiating between vowels can pose a challenge for learners and will take practice. Starting with digraphs that learners can confidently differentiate, even if they cannot accurately reproduce the sounds, is recommended. A key point to reinforce at this stage is that two, three or four letters can represent one sound.

Set Three introduces alternate spelling patterns for the sounds. A key point to reinforce is the concept that a lot of sounds have alternate spellings, such as *ee ea y*, even if those spelling patterns are learnt gradually. It is also worth reinforcing the concept that some spelling patterns represent more than one sound (such as *th, oo, ow*).

The patterns included in the three sets are not the only digraphs and spelling patterns that are needed to read English, but they are the most common and are a good foundation. Further work is needed on less frequent spelling patterns and other irregularly spelt words as learners further develop their language and literacy skills.

Writing

Teaching writing should generally follow the same principles of setting learners up to succeed and not asking learners to complete tasks that they do not have the skills to complete. In practice, this is unrealistic for adults in Australia as every medical centre, dentist, school, real-estate agency, government department, and bank requires forms of some kind to be completed.

Ideally, learners would gradually develop writing skills, and then use them in situations outside the classroom when they were confident and proficient. In reality, learners may be asked to fill in forms before they can write their own name, and a few memorised key words, such as full name, address, country of origin and name of their language in English (exonyms) may be extremely useful. Memorising the prompts for personal information on forms may be less useful simply because there are so many potential variations. Different forms could require: name, given name, first name, full name, preferred name, name as it is written on your proof of ID, maiden name, any names you have been previously known as, surname, second name, or family name.

Within the classroom, writing could parallel development of reading, or there may be minimal emphasis on writing, depending on the needs and interests of learners.

Points to remember

o Writing is a different skill from reading and just because someone can read a given sentence does not necessarily mean that they will be able to write a similar sentence.

o Like reading, writing needs to be explicitly taught.

o Learners should not be asked to write anything that they do not have the skills to complete.

o Learners should be taught that the reading skills they are learning are reversible; if they can decode words, they can learn to generate the sounds to write a word. This will take explicit instruction.

Teaching Spelling

Just because a learner can read a text, it does not mean that they would be able to write an equivalent text. Like most literacy skills, spelling needs to be explicitly taught and, like most literacy skills, a short period of practice frequently is more effective than infrequent extended periods of practice.

o Phonological awareness is necessary for spelling.

o Ensure that learners have a knowledge of phonics and the sounds of English before they are asked to spell words.

o When introducing spelling words, say the word before learners see the printed word. Encourage learners to identify the properties of the word, such as the number of syllables or the first and last sound, before they see the word. The focus should be on the sounds of the word before the learners focus on the written form.

- o If possible, make the spelling program multisensory. Look/cover/write/check relies on short-term visual memory and is unlikely to be particularly effective for learners wanting to learn spelling words.

  Teach learners to:

  - Look at the word.

  - Say the word.

  - Identify any features (number of sounds, number of syllables, a prefix or suffix, irregular spelling patterns and regular sounds).

  - Draw an image associated with the word.

  - Write the word on an alternate surface (markers on the whiteboard, water on a wall).

  - Write the word in a notebook without copying the spelling.

  - Check the spelling.

  - Review the spelling words regularly.

- o Teach orthographic rules, such as the letter *c* usually having a /k/ sound when it is followed by the letter *a, o* or *u,* and a /s/ sound when it is followed by the letter *i, e* or *y.*

- o Teach roots, prefixes, and suffixes of words. This includes the using the prefixes and suffixes to identify parts of speech, such as the suffix *-ly* indicating adverbs, *-ive* indicating adjectives, *-ment* and *-ion* indicating nouns. Understanding that *ed* indicates the tense, even though it may be pronounced /t/, /ed/ or /id/, or that *s* is used to indicate plurals, even though it may be pronounced /z/ as in *bags.*

o Determining learners' spelling words directly from their writing can discourage risk-taking, which should be avoided. If learners are asked to write a piece of writing and know that spelling words will be directly taken from their spelling errors, they are more likely to restrict themselves to words that they can confidently spell, limiting the use of new vocabulary and restricting self-expression.

Handwriting

Some learners may have transferable handwriting skills, while others may not have any experience with writing at all. Like any other skill, the fine-motor skills for writing require practice, and learners who have no experience in writing may have difficulty correctly forming letters even if they can identify the correct formation on a page. It is important to teach a correct pencil grip, even if learners have no desire or need to write for anyone besides themselves, as an incorrect grip can cause a sore hand or arm, which can be a disincentive to attending or participating in class.

The emphasis on handwriting will depend on the needs and goals of the learner; for some learners, handwriting practice is important to enable self-expression and the use of legible written language in the community. For other learners, handwriting is not a priority or may be so difficult, due to hand injuries or other physical traumas, that it is more effective to teach keyboard skills than handwriting. The important aspect is that learners can express their ideas in a form that suits them. Handwriting tends not to be highly valued in Australia outside of classrooms, and many adults rarely handwrite extended texts.

It is worth teaching correct letter formation unless learners are not writing by hand at all because they have other priorities or they are using a computer instead. It is entirely possible to form a letter using multiple strokes of a pen when a standard letter formation requires one or two. For example, it is possible to form a legible letter *e* using three separate strokes of the pen; this might let learners achieve the immediate goal of getting words on a page, but it is much more laborious than writing as efficiently as possible (see Figure 14). Writing with multiple strokes for each letter when one is possible slows down what may already be a slow process. It is worth making it clear to learners that a wide range of letter formation is acceptable (such as *g g g g g g*) and that the aim is not a uniformity of handwriting style so much as ease of expression.

Figure 14: Letter formation

Handwriting practice

Commercially available handwriting books rarely meet the needs of adults, but there are handwriting fonts that can be used to create practice exercises. Handwriting exercises can then be used to reinforce spelling that has been introduced in class or to personalise writing practice for individual learners (see Figure 15).

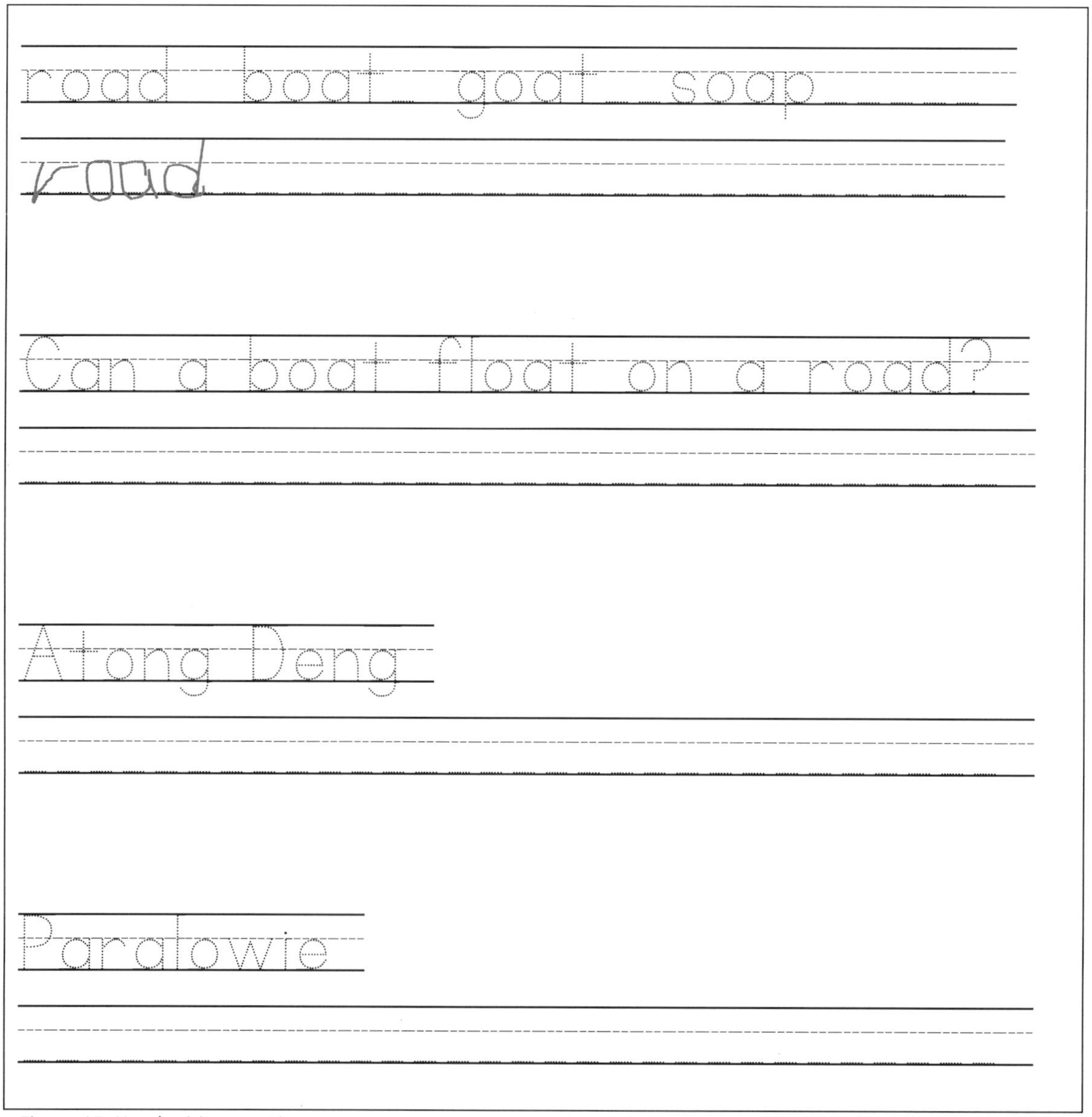

Figure 15: Handwriting practice

Prompting and giving feedback

In a literacy class with English language learners, feedback should allow learners time to self-correct, but otherwise be as immediate as possible (rather than whole-class feedback at the end of the session). Feedback should also be constructive and positive; euphemisms do not help. If a learner reads a sentence, 'It was a dark and stormy nig-hut' and the feedback is, "Good try. You will do better next time", the learner will have no idea what they got right and what they might need to work on. Participation must be encouraged and recognised, but specific feedback is needed for skill development. Adults can be highly skilled at looking for patterns and trying to make sense of the information given; sometimes this can be effective and sometimes it is a strategy that needs to be unlearnt.

If a learner is having difficulty reading a word, the aim is for the instructor to give the minimum amount of help that allows the learner to read the word. If a learner is struggling to read a word or is giving an incorrect response, such as reading *hot* as 'hat', allow about five seconds for the learner to self-correct, then give the minimum guidance required for the learner to read the word correctly.

Initially: 'Look at the letters in the word again.'
Later: 'What **sound** does this make?' (pointing to the letter).

If a learner is really struggling with a word, praise the attempt, give the correct word, and move on. There is no point having the learner give an everlasting string of random guesses.

After the learner has read a text, allow about five seconds for self-correction if needed, and then give feedback on what they got right and what they need to work on next time. Of course, the directions for further action will depend on the structure of the exercise; instructions could be to revise a specific component while other learners have a turn or to practise at home before the next class.

If learners are reading individual words, feedback should include the identification of which sounds the learner read correctly and which sounds they omitted or read incorrectly. For example, "Well done. You got the s, t, a, m sounds right. You missed out the last sound."

"p!.... s t a m p... stamp."

Once learners are reading simple sentences, allowing a brief period of time for self-correction can help learners develop more independence in their reading. Learners should be encouraged to decide if the text they have just read makes sense, and to self-correct, rather than only waiting for feedback from an instructor.

At the sentence level, feedback might direct the learner to a specific word initially, before giving the learner another attempt.

> "Well done. You read the new sounds in 'dark' and 'stormy' very well. Please have a look at the last word while Fatima reads her sentence."

Subsequent feedback might include feedback to the level of sounds.

> "What sound do we get from this?" (Showing 'igh').
> "igh."
> "Good. Have a look at this word again." (Pointing to *night*).
> "n i g h ... No. igh. n igh t. Night."
> "That's right. Well done."

Corrections should be designed to help learners build skills. If a learner cannot complete a task, the corrections should help the learner distinguish sounds. If the target sound is /k/ and the learner nominates the word *city*, remind the learner that they are focussing on sounds, not spelling. "What sound does 'city' start with?" "s" "We are looking for words that start with 'k'."

If the target word is 'slip' and the learner is producing 'sip', feedback should help learners identify the difference between the two sounds. "You said 'sip'. We need the word 'sllllip'. What sound is missing?"

Ideally, learners would start to self-correct their reading, but this generally requires that the vocabulary is known and the concepts are familiar before attempting the reading task. The sentence, 'I went to a hens night on the weekend' may be decodable for a learner, but a culturally-specific pre-marriage party is not appropriate literacy practice unless the concepts and vocabulary have been pre-taught. Learners need to develop reading skills before they can read to learn. It is difficult, if not impossible, to self-correct the reading of a sentence which is not understandable to the reader.

Positive feedback should be given

- Participation: such as "Well done. You gave that a good try."
- Self-correcting: such as "Very good. You corrected yourself."
- Reading a word after help: such as "Good! You worked out that word."
- Reading correctly: "Well done. You read that without any mistakes."

Feedback should always make it very clear exactly what was achieved.

It is worth encouraging a classroom environment where mistakes are not feared and are treated as part of the learning process. Some learners may come from cultures where mistakes in the classroom are cause for deep embarrassment, and it may be worth making it clear to learners what your expectations are regarding participation and achievement (generally participation and mistakes are expected in English language and literacy classrooms in Australia).

Establishing mistakes as part of the learning process

- Make class expectations clear when people start studying. Usually the expectation is that learners will participate and have a try, but it is not a problem if they get an answer wrong.

- Praise attempts in class.

- Recognise that people will be at different levels and what is an easy revision exercise for one person may be very challenging for another learner.

- Draw learners' attention to progress.

- Model an acceptance of mistakes. For example, writing the wrong date on the whiteboard, which was noticed by learners; this can be addressed with a simple acknowledgement of the mistake, thanking the learner who pointed it out, and then moving on to the topic at hand. The idea is to model that mistakes happen without making a drama out of the situation, or implying that mistakes indicate a lack of intelligence.

Key points of giving feedback

- Allow time for learners to think and self-correct.

- Offer suggestions if the learner is struggling.

- Give feedback on what was completed correctly and what needs to be worked on next time.

- Try to create a class environment where mistakes are treated as part of the learning process.

Phonological awareness and Phonemic awareness

Phonological awareness involves a range of skills that relate to the identification and manipulation language. This includes the identification and manipulation of words, syllables, onsets, rimes, and sounds (see Figure 16).

This is a set of skills that is required for, and developed by, literacy development, and for EALD learners, may require some specific practice. For language learners, some phrases that are used or encountered at an early stage in their language acquisition may be formulaic and highly repetitive, such as greetings, introductions and asking for goods and services. It may be very difficult for learners identify the individual words in the connected speech that are used for formulaic greetings and routine conversations. The assistant in the bakery may consistently close a transaction with "Avagooday" [Have a good day], and the bus driver may routinely say "Watchyastep" [Watch your step] as people leave the bus, which makes it very hard to identify word boundaries or individual words in the phrases. People who have a functional command of the English language may still find it very hard to identify features of the language that is being used.

Phonological awareness	Being able to identify and manipulate words, syllables, onsets, rimes, and sounds. Phonological awareness also includes phonemic awareness. Examples of tasks that require phonological awareness are: identifying the number of words in a sentence, the number of syllables in a word, the onset and rime of a word, and the sounds in word.
Phonemic awareness	Being able to identify and manipulate sounds in words. This includes the blending, segmenting, deletion and substitution of sounds in words.

Figure 16: Phonological Awareness and phonemic awareness

Phonemic awareness is a subset of phonological awareness; it is the understanding that spoken language is made up of sequences of individual sounds.

Phonemic awareness is generally both a precursor and an outcome of literacy development: phonemic awareness is a prerequisite of reading, but phonemic awareness skills are in turn further developed by reading. Teaching phonemic awareness should be an ongoing part of literacy development; it is not the end goal in itself but should be part of a broader literacy program. Phonemic awareness is a step in the process of learning to read fluently, and for people learning to read, phonemic awareness is the best single predictor of a learner's successful development of reading skills. There has been significantly less research into adults learning to read in an additional language than the vast body of research into children learning in their first language, but in general, it appears that phonemic awareness will help adults develop emerging literacy skills.

Phonemic skills should be developed systematically. For instructors working with young children in schools, there is a range of well-structured (and some not-so-well structured) phonics programs that instructors can follow that will introduce sounds in an appropriate order and give exercises for developing phonemic awareness. In adult classes with a rolling intake, instructors need to manage the sequence that sounds and tasks are introduced.

The overriding concept is that simple skills should be developed before skills that are more complex are introduced. It is generally easier for learners to break sentences into words than sounds into syllables or to identify the phonemes in words. It is important to keep in mind the difference between developing literacy skills (which involve progressively developing skills) and developing vocabulary and English language skills through reading texts. In the initial stages, it is important that learners are given texts that enable them to develop reading skills. Developing vocabulary from reading can happen once learners have developed skills and confidence in reading.

Developing Phonemic Awareness

It is better to do short PA activities frequently, rather than an extended session infrequently. Like most things that require practice, 15 minutes every day is going to be more effective than one hour once a week. For most children learning to read, a complete phonemic awareness program could be expected to take approximately 20 hours over six months. For adults who are learning to read in an additional language, and who may have erratic attendance patterns, the process could be expected to be slower and require more revision.

Children who have grown up immersed in English will generally differentiate between sounds in English more easily than people learning the language as an adult. Some phonemes may not exist in learners' languages of origin and so may be difficult to distinguish and to produce. Although accurate production of phonemes may assist pronunciation, distinguishing sounds, rather than production, is essential for developing reading skills.

Different languages have specific phonotactic rules about the sound combinations that are possible. English does not allow /ng/ at the start of words. Some languages do not allow specific consonant clusters, or consonant vowel patterns, that are allowed in English. For example, modern standard Vietnamese is a syllable-timed language that allows only nasal consonants, such as /m n/, and unaspirated voiceless plosives /k p t/ in the final position. For Vietnamese speakers, consonant blends pose a specific challenge in language and literacy acquisition. Speakers of other languages face different specific challenges in blending, but targeted phonemic awareness activities may help learners develop skills in sound identification and blending.

Ideally, instructors should be aware of the phonemes that are, or are not, present in the learners' language of origin, although in classes with learners from a range of linguistic backgrounds this may not be possible. There are also some languages and dialects that have not been documented, making phoneme identification difficult for instructors. Where possible, drawing learners' attention to sounds that are present in English but not in their languages of origin can help identify areas of potential difficulty. Helping learners identify phonemes that vary between their languages of origin and English can also significantly help learners, for example, the /r/ that is produced in one language may be considerably different from another language.

Most of the phonemic awareness exercises in the following section can be used as a warm-up or a filler at the end of a lesson and may be complementary to pronunciation activities. Learners who are developing English language skills may not be able to reproduce the sounds studied, but at this stage, it is more important that learners can discriminate between sounds, even if they cannot reproduce the sounds.

Games can be just as useful for adults as for children in learning to read and speak English. Adults may want to understand the purpose of what is studied in the classroom more than young children, but games can be a valuable form of practice, as well as being a useful classroom management tool (bored learners are going to start thinking about lunch or their shopping list, rather than concentrating on some arcane aspect of English spelling). People in the class may have come from a country with a significantly different academic culture, and even if they had no direct experience of that academic culture themselves, there can sometimes be shared understandings within a culture of what is involved with learning and education. Some learners may have very strong ideas of what is involved in studying in a class environment, which may be instructor-centred to the extent that the instructor dispenses information that learners should memorise. Some people may state that "Games are for children. I want to learn English". In this situation, it may be more appropriate to call the task an 'activity' or 'practice', rather than a 'game'.

Adult learners, who may like to see a direct link between tasks and developing skills, may feel frustrated if they are told a speaking exercise is to help them with reading because they cannot see a direct link between the two skills. Those learners may be much more willing to participate if the exercise is linked to pronunciation or listening skills, where there appears to be a much more direct connection between the task and the aims.

It is important that words that are used in the classroom are meaningful to learners, so although some words may fit the phonological pattern for the target language, they might not be part of the learners' current vocabulary and so may not be appropriate for developing phonemic awareness skills. The words *din* or *sod* might be phonemically simple, but if the word is not part of learners' vocabulary, ideally alternative words should be selected. Once exercises have been completed, it is useful for learners to use words in context. For example, learners who have differentiated between the words *rice* and *ice* could use the words in sentences or sentence completion.

The emphasis for these activities should be on sounds and speaking rather than writing and spelling. Writing may be required for keeping score in an exercise, but the emphasis should be on sound and linking those sounds to letters, rather than vocabulary development or sentence construction. Although sounds need to be linked to letters, these are not spelling or writing activities.

Although using a range of activities can provide alternative means of skill practice and variety in the classroom, it can be useful to use the same activities with different sounds or target words as learners' proficiency increases. As learners become confident in their ability to complete the task, they may focus more on the sounds rather than the structure of the exercise.

Learners will need to hear most sounds multiple times, not just once, before they can attempt to differentiate pairs or identify sounds. It is very important to model activities, sometimes repeatedly, showing learners exactly how to perform the task as instructions or descriptions of the language feature being identified or manipulated may not be meaningful to learners. For example, learners may be able to easily understand the concept of initial sounds, but an exercise with final or medial sounds may require more demonstrations and examples.

The same materials can be used for a range of activities in the classroom. Useful props and tools include picture cards that can be used for multiple exercises (initial sounds, final sounds, sounds in any position within the word, odd one out exercises), and sound cards can be a very useful tool for manipulating print (blending, segmentation, deletion, and manipulation of sounds).

Ideally, tasks would be linked back to printed letters. The linking of sounds to letters might be through learners using sound cards, summary words written on the whiteboard at the end of an exercise, or any other method that is appropriate for the class. For example, when playing 'I spy/ I can see', learners may be asked to show the appropriate sound card before making guesses.

Key points

- Phonemic awareness is a key skill required for, and developed by, reading.

- A little practice often is more effective than infrequent extended practice.

- Skills practice should start simply and increase in complexity.

- The difficulty of identifying and manipulating specific sounds will be influenced by learners' languages of origin.

Phonological Awareness: Sequencing

Some sounds are more complex to identify and manipulate. In general, initial sounds are easier to identify and manipulate than final or medial sounds. Continuants, such as /s m l/, are easier to identify than brief sounds, such as stops like /t k g/. Some sound pairs are more difficult to differentiate than others. For people who have grown up speaking English, some of these sounds include:

/k/ and /g/	/f/ and /v/
/f/ and /th/	/p/ and /b/
/t/ and /d/	

These sounds are similar so they can be harder to differentiate. For people who are learning to speak English as an additional language, that list of difficult sounds may be added to with sounds that are not present in their language of origin. In particular, vowels can be difficult to distinguish and may require specific attention and revision.

The tasks that are used in the classroom should start simply and build skills systematically. Learners who cannot distinguish /t/ in *tip* will face even more difficulty distinguishing /t/ in *strip*. Consonant blends, particularly stops, in the final position (such as /pt/ in *slept*) can be very hard for learners to identify and manipulate. The table below (Figure 17) shows the factors that determine the complexity of phonological features for people learning to read.

There is a large range of phonemic awareness activities in the next section. This is not intended as a specific program so much as giving a range of options that can be used or adapted to help learners develop skills in identifying and manipulating sounds. Because these are phonemic awareness activities, not reading activities, the vocabulary used should be chosen according to the needs of learners in sound blending or segmenting, not their reading. For example, learners may be able to decode little more than CVC words but may be able to differentiate between /s/ and /sh/.

Phonological awareness

Factor	Simpler		More complex	
Size of the phonological unit	Break sentences into words	Break words into syllables	Break words and syllables into phonemes	
Number of phonemes in the word	short words such as on, at, bag		Longer words such as drink, truck, stamp	
Phoneme position in words	Initial consonants /m/ in mug /b/ in big	Final consonants /m/ in sum /b/ in tub	Middle consonants /m/ in smash /b/ in stumble	
Consonants or vowels	Consonants		Vowels	
Phonological properties of words	Continuants such as /f/ /h/ /l/ /m/ /n/ /o/ /r/ /s/ /sh/		stops such as /b/ /d/ /g/ /k/ /p/ /t/	
Consonants/ consonant blends	single consonants /s/ in six	blended consonants with continuous sounds /s/ in slow	blended consonants with a stop /s/ in spot	blended consonants with two stops /t/ in adapt
Number of consonants	single consonants /t/ in tip	two blended consonants /t/ in trip	three blended consonants /t/ in strip	
phonemic complexity of the word	short, simple words with two or three phonemes sit, bag, on		longer words with three or more phonemes - splash, scream, straw	
Complexity of blends	blends with only continuous sounds fl, fr, sl, sm, sn, sr		blends with stops bl, br, cr, dr, gr, sc, st, tr	

Figure 17: Phonemic awareness

Hierarchy of phonemic awareness tasks

	Activities	Example
Rhyme Awareness	Identify words that rhyme	Which words rhyme: cat, mug, hat (cat, hat)
	Produce words that rhyme	Tell me a word that rhymes with 'tag' (bag, rag)
Phoneme Awareness	Identify the beginning sound of a word	What sound does 'fish' start with? (f)
	Identify the ending sound of a word	What does 'fan' end with? (n) What is the last sound in 'bus' (s)
	Identify the middle sound of a word	What is the middle sound in 'bag' (a)
Segmenting	Segments sentences into words	Count the words in a sentence. I went to the beach yesterday. (6 words)
	Segment words into syllables	Count the syllables in 'breakfast' (2), in 'Elizabeth' (4)
	Segment words into sounds	What are the sounds in 'man'? (m a n)
Blending Activities	Blend syllables into words	What is the word? sham poo (shampoo)
	Blend sounds into words	What is the word? f r o g (frog)
Manipulation	Delete syllables from words	Say 'handbag' without bag (hand) Say 'running' without run (ing)
	Substitute syllables in words	Say farmer. Change er to ing (farming)
	Delete sounds from words	Say clock. Say clock without the /k/ sound.
	Substitute sounds in words	Change the s in sink to p (pink) Change the u in bug to a (bag)

Figure 18: Hierarchy of phonemic awareness tasks

Phonemic awareness exercises

What words start with /__/?
Process: Tell the class a beginning sound. They repeat the sound and then give you a word that starts with that sound.
Example: "What word starts with the /r/ sound?" The learners repeat the sound /r/ and then say a word such as *red, rent* or *rice*.
Materials: none

What words start with /__/? - Team variation
Process: Divide the class into two or three teams. Teams need to draw as many items starting with a given sound as they can within a time limit. The team with the most items drawn wins.
Example: "What words start with the /b/ sound?" Learners need to graphically represent as many words as they can.
Note: This is not a spelling or writing exercise, it is an opportunity for learners to brainstorm as many words starting with a given sound as they can. *Break* could be represented by a coffee mug or '11am', if that is meaningful to the learners.
Materials: Whiteboard and markers for teams.

Find the same sounds
Process: Learners identify a common phoneme in a set of words.
Example: "What is the sound that is the same in *rice, red* and *road*?" (/r/)
Extension: This can be adapted to be more challenging as learners develop skills and confidence in identifying sounds.
Options: The same exercise can be used with initial (*man, meat, milk*), final (*join, drain, bean*), or medial sounds (*road, home, toast*), or sounds anywhere in the word (*brush, shop, mushroom*).
Materials: Sets of words at the appropriate level.

Words in a sentence

Process: Say sentences to the class. Learners should tap with their pens the number of words that they hear.

Example: I catch the bus to class (six taps). I like eating rice and vegetables (six taps).

Options: Words can be tapped with a pen or pencil, clapped out, or ask learners to raise a finger, depending on learner preferences.

The same process can be useful for counting syllables, but make sure that you clearly model expectations if you are using similar exercises for sounds, syllables and words.

The same task can be used with very simple sentences, or with longer sentences as skills develop.

Materials: Sentences at the appropriate level for the class.

I went shopping

Process: A learner completes the phrase "I went shopping and I bought ..." with a word beginning with /a/. The next learner completes with a sound beginning with /b/. Subsequent learners continue the sequence.

Example: "I went shopping and I bought some apples." Next learner, "I went shopping and I bought some bananas."

Option: Rather than completing the task in alphabetical order, learners can be allocated sounds on flashcards, which allows the instructor to avoid or emphasise certain sounds.

Materials: None required but visual prompts may help learners think of words. Flashcards may help with sound allocation.

What is the last sound?

Process: The learner identifies the final sound of the word given by the instructor.

Example: "What is the last sound in *him*?" The learner repeats the word *him* and then says /m/.

Note: This is more challenging than identifying the initial sounds.

Options: This exercise can be used with words that are more complex as skills develop.

Materials: List of words with relevant sounds.

Blending

Process: Learners blend sounds together.

Example: What word would you get if you put these sounds together?

        /g/ /r/ /ow/ (grow)

        /s/ /oo/ /n/ (soon)

Options: This exercise can use short words, or longer words as learners' skills develop.

Note: This will take considerable modelling and support for learners.

Materials: A list of words at the appropriate level. Some learners may prefer to complete this task with sound cards so that they can physically manipulate letters before giving a verbal answer.

I Spy the Sound

Process: In this variation of the 'I Spy' game, you spy a word that starts with a given sound. For language learners, it may be more appropriate to play "I can see", rather than "I spy".

Example: "I can see something that starts with /p/. What can I see?" Learners need to say the sound /p/ as they look around and find 'pen', 'page' or 'picture'.

Note: Some learners may say 'phone' or 'photo'. Let the learner know that *phone* is spelt with a 'ph' but the sound is /f/. Remind the learner that they are looking for something that begins the /p/ sound and ask the learner to repeat the sound.

Options: This exercise can be used with words that are more complex as skills develop. The exercise can also be used with final or medial sounds with confident learners, such as, "I can see something that ends with t" (belt), or "I can see something that has an ai sound in the middle" (rain).

Materials: None

Rhyming

Process: Show learners what is meant by rhyming words (mug, bug, dug, rug). The onset and rime can be colour-coded on the whiteboard if that helps learners. Say a word like 'sat' and see how many rhyming words the learners can say. The instructor could keep score for individual learners or teams if you feel like making it a competition. Nonsense-words with the appropriate sounds can be accepted if you choose. The emphasis is on sounds, rather than vocabulary.

Example: "What rhymes with sat?" "hat, mat, pat, cat..."

Note: Rhymes will need to be repeatedly demonstrated because learners will often simply give responses that start with the same sound.

Materials: Lists of rhyming sets of words for demonstrations.

Rhyming II

Process: Give learners a set of words and ask them to identify which words rhyme.

Example: "Which words rhyme? rain, cane, late, main."

Note: This is a listening exercise with the aim to identify patterns and exceptions, and so although it may be preferable if learners are familiar with the vocabulary, it is not essential.

Extension: Ask learners why the odd one out does not rhyme (it ends with *ate*, not *ain*).

Materials: Sets of rhyming and contrasting words.

Rhyming III

Process: Show learners a set of 3-5 pictures and ask them to identify the words, and ask learners to identify which words rhyme.

Example: "Look at the pictures. Which words rhyme?" (show a picture of a bee, flower, tree).

Note: Because learners need to generate the vocabulary for this exercise, it is important that learners are familiar with the vocabulary.

Extension: Ask learners why the odd one out does not rhyme (it ends with *er*, not *ee*).

Materials: Sets of pictures of rhyming and contrasting sounds

Same or different - I

Process: Give each learner a handout with the numbers 1- 10 and **same** - **different**, or a graphic indicator for each, depending on the language level of the class. Demonstrate to learners to circle 'same' if the sounds are the same (/t/, /t/) or different (/m/, /t/).

Example: "Number one /b/ /g/. Number two /m/ /m/.

Note: This is a particularly flexible exercise given that the sounds can vary from simple to complex.

Materials: Handouts with: 1) same   different
                                2) same   different
                                3) …

One of these things doesn't belong

Process: Show the learners three – five pictures. Ask learners to name the pictures. It is important to get learners to identify the pictures, as the same drawing could potentially be named as a beach, sand, fun, hot, summer, water, etc. Ask learners to say the words and then identify which one 'does not belong'. For beginning learners, the pictures might be a snake, sausage, <u>carrot</u>, sandwich.

Example: "Listen to the starting sounds. Which one does not belong?"

Note: If you don't tell learners exactly what to listen for, some learners will look for thematic patterns. You may need to reinforce the aspect that they are concentrating on, otherwise some learners will think that 'snake' is the odd word out as the others are food. This will take a lot of modelling.

Working with pictures has the advantage that words that are part of learners' vocabulary but they are unable to read can be included in the activity.

Extension: Once learners are familiar and confident with the task, ask learners why that word does not belong. Learners then need to articulate the specific differences between words ("One word starts with /k/, the other words start with /s/").

Materials: Sets of pictures

Colour rhymes

Process: The instructor colour-codes the onset and rime on the whiteboard, and then demonstrates how to generate new words.

Example: "This is the word sit. What are some other words that rhyme with sit?"

Note: Avoid using red and green as contrasting colours as there may be some learners who have difficulty differentiating those colours.

Working with onset and rime can be part of a phonemic awareness program, but is not an effective reading strategy in itself. There are some literacy programs that place a great deal of emphasis on teaching onset/ rime, but this has been found to be an ineffective strategy in isolation from a broader program.

Materials: Whiteboard and markers

Same or different - II

Process: Stick a graphic indicator 'same' on one wall and 'different' on the wall opposite. Demonstrate turning to face 'same' in response to hearing two sounds that are the same, and turning to face 'different' in response to different sounds. Ask learners to stand up, facing the front. Give two sounds and prompt learners to turn the direction they think is correct. Learners to sit down if they are incorrect.

Example: /s/ /s/ (learners face 'same'). /t/ /g/ (learners face 'different').

Note: This version can be useful if learners need a break from sitting down.

Materials: Large graphic indicators to stick on the wall.

Counting sounds

Process: Learners count the number of sounds in a word.

Example: "s (finger up), i (finger up), t (finger up). How many sounds?" "3"

"r" (tap table), ai (tap table), n (tap table). How many sounds?" "3"

Options: Show the learners how to raise a finger, move a counter, or tap a pen for each sound.

This exercise can use one-syllable words, or longer words as learners develop more skills.

Materials: Counters if choosing that option.

Find the error

Process: The instructor says a phrase or simple sentence with a sound changed. Ask learners to identify the incorrect sound.

Example: "I cooked some rice in a big mot".

Note: For EALD learners, make sure that learners are confident with the concepts and vocabulary.

Materials: Sentences at the right level for the class.

Back to back dictation

Process: Learners to sit back to back. One learner says a sound (of their choice, or from a list supplied by the instructor, depending on the class), the other learner to write down the appropriate letter.

Example: "One /s/. Two /b/.... "

Note: The advantage of sitting back to back is that learners lose visual cues and need to focus on sounds.

This exercise is about writing down sounds, and so writing the word *boat* as *bote* is meeting the aims of the task.

Options: This can be used with single sounds, or sounding out entire words, such as *shop* or *rainbow*, for more advanced learners.

Materials: List of sounds or words that can be supplied to learners, and a learner notebook for writing responses.

Not rhymes

Process: If learners are confident with rhymes, this can be used as an extension. Give learners two words, ask if they rhyme, and if not, why not. This should be practice in distinguishing differences between words.

Example: "Do 'mop' and 'mix' rhyme?" "Why not?"

Materials: Word pairs

Find the vowel

Vowels can be difficult for people learning to read and can be particularly difficult for EALD learners developing literacy skills in an additional language.

Process: Give learners a pair of words (hat, hot). Ask learners to repeat the words. Ask learners to identify the vowels.

Example: "Listen to the words. /ban/ /sat/. What are the middle sounds?

Note: Medial sounds are more difficult than initial or final sounds and should only be introduced once learners are confident identifying sounds at the start and end of words.

Materials: word pairs at the right level for the class.

Find the difference

Process: Give learners pairs of words, ask them to repeat the words and then identify the difference. Choose words that are appropriate for the skills of the learners.

Example: "bay, day. What is the difference?"
"deep, beep. What is the difference?"

Options: This can be used with pairs with different initial, final, or middle sounds, depending on the class, with pairs such as such as 'bad, bat' or 'feel, foil'.

Materials: Word pairs at the right level for the class.

Tell me the sounds

Process: Give the learners an appropriate word and ask them to segment the sounds in the word.

Example: "Tell me the sounds in *sit*". The learner should say "/s/ /i/ /t/". "Tell me the sounds in 'chop'", the learner should say /ch/ /o/ /p/.

"Tell me the sounds in the word *money*." The learner should say /m/ /u/ /n/ /ee/.

Options: This exercise can be used with longer words as skills develop.

Materials: Words at the right level for the class.

Dictation

Process: Learners should write down the sounds, phrases, or sentences that are dictated. The sounds or phrases will need to be repeated at least twice.

Example: 1) /s/ /s/
2) /r/ /r/
3) /m/ /m/
4)…

Options: This exercise can be adapted from beginner to advanced learners as skills develop.
Single sounds: /t/ /m/ /sh/ /ai/
Words by sound: /sh/ /u/ /t/
Words: *gate, soap*).

Note: This is a highly flexible exercise as it can easily be adapted to the level of the class.

Materials: Sounds, words or sentences at the right level for the class.

Compound word deletion
Process: learners delete part of a compound word.
Example: "Say 'pancake'. Say it again, don't say 'pan'".
Materials: a list of compound words.

Syllable deletion
Process: Learners delete part of a word.
Example: "Say complain. Say it again but don't say 'com'".
Note: This is a more challenging task and will take a lot of modelling and practice to achieve.
Materials: a list of multi-syllable words.

Sound deletion
Process: Learners delete a sound from a word.
Example: "Say the word 'sat' without the /s/".
"Say the word 'hand' without the /d/.
Note: Sound deletion and manipulation will take a lot of modelling, and even if learners can blend and segment relatively complex words, deletion is a more demanding task and should start very simply before gradually increasing in complexity as learners' skills develop.
Options: This is a flexible exercise because the same task can be used with sounds in different positions. The progression of sound deletions should be:

      Initial positions
      Final positions
      Initial blends
      Medial positions
      Final blends

Learners who can successfully delete sounds from words may still find it difficult to identify the sounds that have been deleted.
Materials: A word list for sound deletion. Some learners prefer to complete this task with sound cards so that they can physically manipulate letters before giving a verbal answer.

Swapping sounds

Process: Tell learners which specific sounds you want them to change in a word.

Example: "We have the word 'tap'. What word will we have if we change the /t/ to a /l/?

"We have the word 'dust'. What word will we have if we change the /d/ to a /r/?

Note: Swapping sounds will need a lot of modelling.

Options: This task can be completed with initial (*sand, band*), final (*trim, trip*) or medial sounds (*lamp, lump*).

Materials: A word list for sound manipulation. Some learners may prefer to complete this task with sound cards so that they can physically manipulate letters before giving a verbal answer.

Picture sort

This is a good introductory rhyming activity.

Process: Give learners a mixed set of pictures. Ask learners to name the pictures, then learners should sort sets of pictures into rhyming categories (fox, box/ cake, rake).

Note: In the initial stages, it is important to get learners to identify the pictures first, as the same drawing could potentially be named as *lunch, sandwich, food, meal*, etc.

Options: As learners become more confident, they can identify both the words and the rhymes.

Materials: Sets of pictures illustrating rhyming words.

Word grids

Process: Learners fill in the grid with one sound from a word in each box.

Note: It is possible to make the task easier by giving a grid with the corresponding number of sounds (as for *train*, below), or more challenging by giving a grid with more squares than the number of sounds required (as for *book*, below).

Materials: List of target words, a photocopied sheet with a grid.

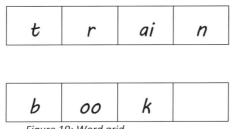

Figure 19: Word grid

Rhyming Sentence completion

Process: Say a sentence to the class but do not say the final word. Ask learners to complete the sentence with a rhyming word.

Example: "I can see a black _____" (pack, rack, sack)
"There is a cap on a ____" (map, tap, lap)

Note: Make sure learners are confident with generating rhyming words before attempting this exercise.

EALD learners may struggle with the concept of multiple correct answers, and nonsensical sentences. It may be worth following up the exercise with class discussion. "*A car in a jar.* Does that make sense?"

Options: Some learners may feel more confident completing the exercise if the response required involves selecting an appropriate answer. Picture cards with a mixture of sounds may provide support, for example, the sentence "In my bag there is a _____" could be supported with pictures of a banana, a plate, and a flag.

Materials: Sentences with rhymes. Optional materials: picture cards.

Multisensory word grids
Process: Learners fill in the grid with words supplied by the instructor. Learners should say the target word before they write it and generate a rhyming word.

Materials: List of target words, a photocopied sheet with a grid.

Picture	Word	Rhyming word
	house	*mouse*

Figure 20: Multisensory word grid

Picture Card Snap
Process: Learners play Snap with sound and picture cards.

Example: A learner puts down a picture of a fish. The next learner puts down a picture of a pen. The next learner puts down the card .p.

A learner calls "Snap!" and collects the cards.

Options: This exercise can be adapted to make it more challenging. The sound matching can target the initial sound, any sound within the word, final, or medial sounds.

Materials: A set of picture and sound cards.

Add a sound

Process: Learners should add a sound to a word.

Example: "Say 'pain.' Now say it with /t/ at the end."

Options: It is possible to use the same exercise with initial sounds (pain + s, spain), final (pain + t, paint), or initial blend sounds (pain + l, plain, or suck + t, stuck).

Materials: A list of appropriate words. Some learners may prefer to complete this task with sound cards so that they can physically manipulate letters before giving a verbal answer.

Onset matching

Process: Learners should decide if onsets are the same or different.

Example: "Do these words start with the same sound? 'shoe, shop?' (yes) 'clap, frog' (no).

Materials: a list of appropriate words. Some learners may prefer to complete this task with sound cards so that they can physically manipulate letters before giving a verbal answer.

Isolation of sounds

Process: Learners should identify the sound at the beginning of the word.

Example: "What sound can you hear at the beginning of 'snake'?" "What sound can you hear at the being of 'drink'?"

Materials: List of words at the appropriate level

Isolation of sounds II

Process: Learners should identify the sounds in a word.

Example: "What sounds can you hear in the word 'skin'?" (/s/ /k/ /i/ /n/) "What sounds can you hear in the word 'lock'?" (/l/ /o/ /k/)

Options: This can be made more challenging by using longer words.

Materials: List of words at the appropriate level

Making words

Process: Give learners a set number of sound cards and direct them to make as many words as they can from the given letters.

Example: From *a l m r s t* sound cards learners could make the words *am, arm, arms, art, last, malt, mast, mat, ram, rat, rats, salt, sat, slam, smart, star, tar, tram, trams*, etc.

Note: This task is much easier with cards that learners can manipulate rather than with the letters only written on the whiteboard.

Materials: sets of sound cards

Word changing

Process: Learners should manipulate words using sound cards.

Example: "Make the word *bag*" (learners put down sound cards to show the word). "Now change the word to make *rag*".

Options: This task can target initial, final or medial sounds.

Materials: Sound cards, and a list of word chains.

Adapting phonemic awareness tasks

The aim in phonemic awareness exercises is to develop skills in sound identification or manipulation rather than to finish specific tasks simply for the sake of completion. Exercises can be adapted to suit the needs and interests of learners. While it is useful to use a range of phonemic awareness tasks in class to provide variety and to practice specific skills, such as blending or segmenting, it is also a good idea to adapt the same task to more challenging language as learners' skills develop. Using the same task means that learners are familiar with the expectations of the task and can concentrate on the language or skills involved, rather than trying to focus on the process of completing the task.

Most phonemic awareness exercises can be adapted to suit the needs of beginner to advanced learners; a word game that suits beginner learners that requires the identification of beginning sounds can be made much more challenging by using medial sounds. For example, "Which word does not belong: lake, rain, pay, hat?" It is also possible to use an exercise to blend simple words, and then later use the same task to blend words that are more complex. Similarly, most of the phonemic awareness tasks can be adapted to suit team games. Instead of individual learners giving responses, most tasks can be adapted to suit team competitions. For learners who lack confidence, team exercises can be a valuable tool for gaining practice without feeling like the attention is solely on them.

Rebuses

Rebuses are words and sentences written using letters, logograms or symbols, and pictures. They have been used as puzzles and riddles in different countries since the fifteenth century; they are not just a product of the iPhone era.

It is not a good idea to teach language learners that the way to write 'See you later' is CUL8R, but rebuses can be useful for phonemic awareness activities. This is just one more way of practising language skills.

Figure 21: Rebus

Another use of rebuses is enabling learners to work with sentences on relevant topics when they are still developing reading skills. Pictures can be substituted for words that contain spelling patterns that have not yet been studied, which means that sentences that are relevant to learners can be used for a reading exercise. One note of caution: symbols are culturally specific, and a graphic indicator that is commonly understood in Australia may not be recognised by people from another cultural or language background. If possible, photos that are specific to learners or the class are ideal.

Figure 22: Rebus puzzles

Special words

'Special words', or irregular words, are ones that don't fit regular spelling patterns in some way, for example, the word *was* is pronounced /woz/ not /wass/. The term that is used doesn't really matter, but it should be consistent between instructors and classes. As long as there is consistency between classes, there is no reason they couldn't be called 'green words', printed on tinted green paper and pinned on the wall if that suits the class. For English language learners, it might be helpful to avoid calling the spelling 'irregular' because that is a term that is also applied to verb tenses. It is worth avoiding calling these 'difficult' words; they might need some special attention but are no more difficult than other words.

Make sure that learners can use the words before they are introduced as spelling words. For example, there is no point introducing the word *could* as a spelling word if learners are not familiar with the vocabulary and modal sentence construction ('You could borrow a DVD from the library'), or teaching the spelling of the word *as* before learners are able to use comparatives ('The pumpkin was as big as a soccer ball').

Explicitly teach learners to read specific irregular words before they are expected to read them independently. This means instruction in reading the word, revision and practice. Similarly, learners should learn to read words before attempting to write the same words.

Teaching irregular words

Make sure that learners are able to decode at least CVC words before introducing irregular spelling patterns. Many adults develop ineffective reading strategies when they are presented with reading that is beyond their reading abilities, and decoding is important to reinforce before introducing words that do not follow the same patterns.

Introduce the idea that some words are decodable, but some don't follow the same rules, if possible using a highly familiar name or word, such as *was*, as an example. Introduce the idea that English has about 80% regular spelling, 20% irregular spelling, but often that 20% are the high-frequency words.

Steps for teaching irregular words

- Use the word in context.

- Identify the sounds that are regular and which are irregular; there are almost always some regular sounds in irregularly spelt words, and even in less frequent spelling patterns, it is usually not random. For example, in *want*, the /w/ /n/ /t/ are regular, only the *a* having an /o/ sound is a less frequent spelling pattern, and even that is not random, simply less common.

- Learners say the word.

- Learners copy the word, then cover the word, write it again, and check the spelling.

- If possible, make the spelling practice multisensory.

- Practice at intervals. Introducing a word and never revisiting it again makes it improbable that the word will be retained.

Introduce words at a pace that lets learners remember the words. For some classes, that will mean about two or three new words a week, as well as revision of words from previous weeks.

Special word list

the	which	more
be	go	said
to	me	have
of	when	put
a	time	many
I	no	is
he	people	into
you	your	before
do	some	live
his	other	are
they	only	here
we	come	goes
she	two	four
one	want	little
all	because	was
there	any	were
their	give	where
what	don't	would
so	does	could
who	I'm	as

Some of these words are relatively easy to spell, such as *a*, *I*, and *me*, but it is still worth reviewing them as an irregular spelling pattern to draw attention to the differences from more regularly spelt words.

Mnemonics

Mnemonics are phases and sentences that help learners remember spelling that is more difficult or to differentiate between homophones such as *there, their* and *they're*. It helps if the phrases are meaningful to the learners; there is no point referencing daffodils in a phrase if learners have never seen one, and simply showing a picture of a daffodil does not make the flowers meaningful to learners. It is also useful if learners can be reminded of the phase if needed, and so individually relevant phrases require learners to have the study skills to record and retrieve their own phrases.

Drawing images on the words that need to be remembered can be helpful if the images are relevant to the learner, such as a visual reminder that of a narrative which ended with '...I went too' (see Figure 23).

Using mnemonics is a strategy that should be used sparingly; too many sentences and phrases to remember makes them an ineffective memory tool for spelling.

because:	big elephants can always understand small elephants

Figure 23: Mnemonics

Drawing the skills together

The Big Five reading skills are:
- o Phonemic Awareness
- o Phonics Instruction
- o Fluency
- o Vocabulary
- o Comprehension

The emphasis on different skills will shift over time as reading proficiency develops (see Figure 24).

Shift in emphasis in skill instruction

Phonemic Awareness	There will be greater emphasis on phonemic awareness in the early stages of literacy instruction, but pronunciation development may continue as learners progress with their English language studies.
Phonics Instruction	There will be greater emphasis on phonics in the early stages of literacy instruction, but spelling programs may continue as learners' progress with their English language studies.
Fluency	There will be greater emphasis on fluency in later stages of literacy instruction.
Vocabulary	Vocabulary instruction is important in both the early and later stages of literacy development, although the methods of instruction may shift as learners develop skills. The emphasis may shift from instructor-determined vocabulary sets, which are taught using realia and images, to learner-determined vocabulary or thematically related vocabulary.
Comprehension	Comprehension is important in both the early and later stages of literacy development, but the depth of comprehension will change. In the initial stages of literacy development, comprehension will relate to single words. Later stages could relate to critical reading of entire texts or comparisons of texts.

Figure 24: Shift in emphasis in skill instruction

Reading does not just require just one skill; fluent, confident reading requires a range of related abilities. Phonemic awareness is a set of skills that are required for, and developed by, reading but it is not a goal in its own right so much as a set of skills that lay the foundation for reading. Similarly, decoding and phonics skills are useful tools for reading, but ideally, learners would move on to becoming fluent readers who do not need to consciously decode words because their reading skills have become automatic. The emphasis on the instruction in specific skills will shift over time as learners' literacy skills develop (see Figure 24). The strongest predictors of reading comprehension in an additional language are knowledge of the language's grammar, vocabulary knowledge and decoding skills. This does not suggest that other skills can be neglected because the skills are complementary and interrelated.

Reading Practice

Learners will need to practice regularly to maintain and develop literacy skills. It is not enough to simply introduce sounds and spelling patterns in class and then move on; there needs to be regular revision and practice of skills both inside and outside the classroom. Learners need a lot of practice to develop automaticity and fluency; it is not enough to decode words, learners need to practice until they have developed reading skills that are effortless and do not require conscious attention. It is important that practice corresponds to the material studied in class, as it is ineffective to have a well-structured class program and homework that either does not support this class work or undermines the reading strategies by expecting learners to read above their current ability.

Ideally, learners would practice previously studied sounds and spelling patterns as well as newly introduced patterns. Reading a text with a mixture of sounds is much more challenging than reading sentences with an emphasis on one sound. Because this resource has been developed to be used in classes with a rolling intake, it is important to mix the sounds and spelling patterns that are used in reading practice, rather than only reading sets of sentences with the patterns introduced that week. Ideally, learners would practice reading frequently for short periods, not just infrequently for extended periods. Regular short periods of practice may not be possible for adult learners with competing demands on their time, but it is the goal.

Reading practice should be challenging enough to be interesting, but not so hard that it is frustrating or that learners start guessing words based on the initial letter of the word or a picture. Up to ten errors per 100 words is a useful guide in the initial stages of literacy development, but this should reduce as reading skills are developed. Reading texts with more than ten errors per 100 words is too frustrating, and fewer than four challenging words per 100 may be too easy for work in the classroom (although that may be a good level for independent practice). A decreasing rate of errors correlates with increased reading fluency and comprehension; it is hard to make sense of texts while struggling to read individual words. As learners' reading proficiency increases, practice can shift from tightly controlled, decodable texts to texts that are more authentic, but the reading materials should always be within the abilities of learners.

The aims and structure of practice will change over time as skills develop; the task that suits a learner who is starting to decode CVC words would not suit a learner who is aiming to develop reading fluency. Round-robin reading, where each learner in the class reads a section of text, may be an effective way for the instructor to hear each learner and to gauge progress, but it is not efficient practice for a large group of people in a class as each person only reads for a short time.

Reading the same text aloud three or four times may help learners develop fluency more effectively than reading in a round robin or silently. In a large class, it is usually not possible to have all people read the same text repeatedly to the class, and so small groups working together, audio recordings, and practising with people outside the classroom may be more effective.

For adult EALD learners, practice at home may require creativity due to competing demands on time and energy, and the challenge of finding someone to hear reading. The options for regular reading practice outside the classroom will depend on the circumstances of learners. There is a correlation between reading practice and reading fluency, and so it is worth encouraging learners to practice outside the classroom.

Suggested options for practice

o Make reading collaborative. For learners with kindergarten or primary school aged children, reading tasks can be presented as help for their children.

o Help learners identify people in their family or community who can listen to them read at regular intervals. It may be useful to supply a brief summary of the aims of practice (skill development rather than task completion) for the people hearing the reading practice.

o Ideally, learners would get immediate feedback on their reading, but in some circumstances, it might be necessary to have learners read independently at home and get feedback on their reading the next time they are in class.

o Peer teaching; more advanced learners can listen to reading. Peer teaching is not just of benefit to the person practising reading, as giving feedback requires that learners can articulate the specifics of errors and corrections.

o If learners are confident using technology, teach them how to record themselves on their phone or computer so that they can listen to themselves.

Key points

- Frequent practice for short periods is more effective than infrequent extended practice.

- Creativity might be required to help learners get regular practice outside the classroom.

Technology, Apps and Websites

Any information about specific websites or apps is going to be out of date almost as soon as it is written, but some general concepts can be applied:

o Whether learners are using an app, paper and pen, or a stick in the sand, the aim is for learners to develop reading skills. Apps and websites are only useful if they help learners develop the intended skills. Just because something has 'literacy' or 'reading' in the title does not mean that it will necessarily suit the current specific needs of learners.

o There is a huge market for educational apps. Some apps and websites are well designed, but a lot are not, so it is worth checking the content (which specific skills are being targeted, if any) and the design (if it is possible to click through the task without paying attention to the intended content).

o Apps and websites are an international market. Unless the app has been specifically developed for an Australian accent, there will be variation between the sounds in the app and the accent that learners hear every day. It is worth avoiding unnecessary complication, confusion, or learners struggling to complete an exercise because the local pronunciation is considered 'wrong'.

o Some adults in an English or literacy class may be highly proficient in the use of websites and apps, but others may have had minimal exposure to the internet and smart phones. Some learners will need assistance in accessing technology or may find the format more challenging than the content. For some people the use of technology is itself stressful, so rather than being a means of practising new skills, a computer session can be a barrier to participation or a disincentive to attending class.

o Most literacy apps are designed for children so the vocabulary, exercise structure, and visual presentation may not be appropriate for adult learners.

o Technology is sometimes regarded as a means of engaging learners, but a boring spelling exercise is going to be boring on paper or on a website. The exercise itself also needs to be engaging; it is not enough to rely on the medium to make the task interesting.

o Technology is changing rapidly. A few years ago, speech-to-text and text-to-speech functions took a lot of practice to use and had limited applications. Now those functions are easier to use and have improved significantly. This is a function that adult EALD learners may find useful.

o Visual dictionaries can be very useful for language learners, but it is important that the language included on the site matches the local terms. A site that refers to *sweaters, soda, fall* (as a season), *drug store*, or *faucet* is simply going to cause confusion for learners who have learnt that the vocabulary is *jumper, soft drinks, autumn, chemist*, or *tap*. Advanced English language learners may confidently cope with variations between English in different regions, but this should be avoided for learners in the early stages of language and literacy development. This comes back to the idea that there is a difference between vocabulary development and literacy development.

o Check that the app or site can be used independently by learners. A lot of literacy apps have been designed to be used with support from a parent or teacher and so a straightforward exercise, such as matching upper and lower case letters, may require navigating through several sections of a website, or understanding a relatively complex set of instructions.

Case studies

A full-day class: sample day

Time	Task	Details	Notes
9:00am 5 mins	Routine administration		This is a chance to greet people, follow up absences, and congratulate people on milestones such as getting their driver's licence.
5 mins	Check the weather forecast	Check the weather forecast on the Bureau of Meteorology website, projected on the screen. Learners are checking the temperature and using the icons rather than reading the extended text.	A few learners come in late. This is a good chance to revise vocabulary.
10 mins	Review class expectations	Review class expectations relating to attendance, participation and notification of absences – learners to supply the details with prompting.	Having learners supply the details is useful for concept checking, and helps maintain interest for a task that is frequently repeated as learners start throughout the year.
5 mins	Review of sounds	Review of sounds of the alphabet – using A4 flashcards, first time with the whole class calling out sounds, the second time with a nominated learner giving the sound.	Observing the participation of the recommencing and new learners. Easier sounds to be chosen, apparently at random, for specific learners.
5 mins	Review of concept	Review of why it is important to use sounds, not letter names, when reading. Learners to give information when they can.	Decisions will need to be made about the level of support needed for the new learners.

60 minutes	Introduction of three new sounds for the week	Introduce the sound in context, learners to use the sounds and write example words in a wordbook.	
5 mins	Break		
85 mins	Curriculum unit	Teaching related to the academic curriculum, in this case, clothing and expressing preferences. This involves several short tasks.	Teaching with an emphasis on spoken language and visual support. Ideally, learners would read words with spelling patterns that have been introduced, but not words that they do not yet have the skills to decode.
30 mins	Lunch		
12:30pm 5 mins	Warm up	Phonemic awareness task – identifying initial sounds	This is review exercise for some learners and an introduction of concepts for two people.
75 mins	Curriculum unit	Teaching related to the academic curriculum. Several short tasks.	
10 mins	Break		
10 mins	Spelling activity	Review of previous irregular spelling words and introduction of two new words	
20 mins	Handwriting	Handwriting practice using worksheets relating to current vocabulary	This is a low concentration exercise, which is useful towards the end of the day.
10 mins	Revision activity	Revision of sounds, vocabulary and grammar structures that were introduced during the day	

5 mins 2:45pm End of class	Routine administration	Reminders about homework and the coming work.	

Figure 25: Sample day

It is a class that learners attend between one and four days a week, with the specific days attended determined by factors such as childcare availability and units of study that have been completed already. Classes run from 9:00am to 2:45pm. There is rolling intake into the class; some learners have been attending the class for months, and others have started more recently. It is a day around mid-semester, so some learners are familiar with class expectations, the structure of activities and key concepts of decoding and blending words. In the class of twenty learners, two learners are returning after an extended absence due to travel and illness, and two learners are starting today for the first time. The two new learners already have social contacts within their language groups.

About two-thirds of the class is made up of two main language groups, with the remaining learners from other language backgrounds.

Start and finish times, and the length of breaks, are dictated by the organisation. Because the learners have different attendance patterns, it is not feasible to introduce one sound each day, as some learners would consistently miss content covered in class on specific days. For that reason, approximately three sounds are introduced each week, with all three sounds being reviewed each day with a different combination of learners in the class. This is not ideal, but the best option for the class.

A sample tutoring session

Time	Task	Details	Notes
9:50am

10 mins | Mary arrives. | A social catch-up while Ayana gets a drink of water for both of them | |
| 5 mins | Review the practice work that was set. | Ayana reads the practice work that was set last week. She is proud that she has managed to read the text and her confidence in reading is growing. | She is getting more confident in asking questions about the content and structure of texts. Notes are made for future exercises. |
| 5 mins | Phonemic awareness task | Identifying the final sounds in words.

The task is adapted on the spot to make it more challenging, shifting the focus from the final to the medial sounds. | Ayana finds the task, as it was first presented, very easy. She first did a similar exercise with Mary some time ago and says that she has been doing similar exercises with her children in Tigrinya, presenting it as a game to do while they are waiting for a bus. |
10 mins	Introduction of a new spelling pattern; ir.	Introduction of the sound, a discussion around some of the words and Ayana writes some example words her Wordbook.	Only one pattern is introduced at a time. Ayana would prefer more, but she does not retain as much if sounds are introduced too rapidly.
15 mins	Reading practice	The reading includes the sound introduced today and previously studied digraphs.	
2 mins	Ayana checks on her toddler, who is with her husband.		Both the child and husband seem happy, but it is a good reason to take a short break from studying.

20 mins	Vocabulary development	Locating information on a utilities bill, and the difference between 'amount owed' and 'amount owed with pay on time discount'.	Ayana is not able to read every word on the bill, and does not attempt to do so, but she is able to locate specific information. This topic was chosen in response to questions the week before.
5 mins	End of session review and setting of practice work		Ayana frequently asks for more work than she can complete, and the amount of practice work is discussed.
30 mins	Social chat over coffee	Ayana makes the coffee, which is an elaborate process on a burner. This is an opportunity for a social chat and is a much more low-pressure way to practice English than at the desk.	Ayana has questions about content that was in her children's homework, and so the vocabulary development next week will relate to the topic of plants. Reading that vocabulary is beyond Ayana's current abilities, but if it is a nice day, Mary and Ayana will go to the park at the end of the street to look at the trees.

Figure 26: Sample tutoring session

A volunteer tutor, Mary, works with Ayana at her house for one hour a week. Ayana has three young children, one with health issues, and so is unable to attend classes regularly. Mary has been working with Ayana for a little over a year, and she often stays after the formal tutoring session to have a coffee and a chat. Even though the tutoring is highly flexible and responsive to Ayana's needs and interests, there is still a routine of checking material that was set for independent practice, the introduction of new sounds or spelling patterns, and vocabulary development relating to an immediate need or interest.

Because the there is only one learner, there is an opportunity to tailor the tutoring session to her goals and immediate needs. Skills that have already been developed can be quickly revised before moving on to study new skills. Topics that are raised in conversation over coffee are often raised again as part of vocabulary development.

Ayana did not have the opportunity to access formal education in Eritrea and would like to learn as much as possible as quickly as possible, sometimes in unrealistic time-frames, despite finding the intensity of one-to-one tutoring exhausting. Ayana finds it difficult to practice reading and speaking English with people, but she is gradually making contact with other parents at her children's school. She wants her children to learn to speak Tigrinya, and she likes the idea of adapting English language exercises to teach her children Tigrinya. She is not confident practising reading English with her two children who attend primary school, but she does read books in English to her 18 month-old daughter while her other two children are at school.

Ayana sees learning English and learning to read as urgent for her own benefit, having stated, "In Australia, everything is written. In Eritrea, not so much." She would like to study once her children are older, but she is not sure of the area of study that interests her, she simply wants to take every opportunity for education that is offered. She does not currently see much value in writing for self-expression, although she does write down some example words and spelling patterns, her goals are to develop reading, speaking and listening skills.

Class in a community centre: sample session

Time	Task	Details	Notes
3:00pm 5 mins	Greetings, social inquiries about events during the week, and routine administration		There is a strong social aspect to the class, and some learners come early to catch up with friends
10 mins	Phonemic awareness task	Differentiation of vowels: an aspect of language that many of the learners find difficult.	The exercise is linked to pronunciation, which is regarded as an immediate goal by some of the learners in the class.
45 mins	Introduction of two new sounds for the week	Introduce the sound in context, learners use the sounds and spelling patterns, and some learners write the sound and example words.	
Five-minute break			
40 mins	Vocabulary development	Teaching vocabulary related to a thematic topic, in this case, neighbourhood disputes such as barking dogs and cars blocking access to driveways, with an emphasis on roleplays and spoken language exercises.	The topic was chosen in response to learner interests and needs, and continues a class theme of using appropriate language in different situations.
10 mins	Introduction of two new spelling words and review of four previous words.	Group exercise	This is presented as a reminder rather than a review of spelling because some learners in the class find spelling particularly stressful.

5 mins	An informal recap of the session	Details for the recap supplied by learners.	
	Homework distribution and reminders		
5:00pm			
End of session			
30 mins	Some learners stay for a cup of tea.		

Figure 27: Sample session at a community centre

It is a very informal class in a community centre that is held for two hours once a week. The aims are to help develop language and literacy skills, but there is no specified curriculum, and topics for study are determined by learner interest and need. Theoretically there is a rolling intake, although the class has been stable for some months.

The class is made up of both men and women from a range of countries and ages, although there are no women with young children in the class as those learners are in a different class. Some learners have been in Australia for years and speak some English, but are now looking to develop their skills after a back injury or change of job. A few of the people in the class have worked on construction sites and have learnt a lot of spoken English, and now have the aim to develop language skills for more formal situations.

Most people in the class regularly attend, although a few people come when their work schedule permits. The social aspect of the class is particularly important to several people in the class, who regularly arrive early or stay for a cup of tea after the session has finished.

Practice materials are distributed each week, and some learners practice reading at home, but other people tend not to practice outside the classroom.

Learner tracking

Name	At commencement										After studying			
	Sounds							Letter formation						
	Knows no sounds or names	Knows some sounds of the alphabet	Knows all sounds of the alphabet	Knows some letters names	Knows all letters names	Mixes letter names and sounds	Knows some digraphs	Cannot form letters	Can form some letters	Can form letters	Knows the sounds of the alphabet	Cannot form letters	Can form some letters	Can form letters
Mai				✓					✓		✓		✓	
Khadija						✓		✓			✓		✓	
Marco		✓		✓						✓	✓			✓

Figure 28: Skills at commencement example

Name	ai		ee		ie		oe		th		ch		oi		sh		ou			
	Introduction	Review	Introduction	Review	Introduction	Review	Introduction	Review	Introduction	Review	Introduction	Review	Introduction	Review	Introduction	Review	Introduction	Review	Introduction	review
Mai	✓	✓	✓	✓	✓	✓					✓	✓	✓							
Khadija											✓	✓	✓	✓	✓	✓	✓	✓		
Marco							✓	✓	✓	✓	✓	✓	✓	✓	✓					

Figure 29: Progress tracking example

Word lists and resources

Many of the following word lists include vocabulary that will be beyond the abilities of language and literacy learners. These lists could have a role in some phonemic awareness exercises, but they should be used with caution.

These lists and resources are useful for phonemic awareness tasks, but they are not intended as complete lists of a class of words so much as suggestions to get instructors started. These sets are not intended for learner memorisation.

The following resources could be used for:
- o Introducing specific sounds and spelling patterns.
- o Phonemic awareness exercises
    - ▪ Rhyme identification and generation
    - ▪ Sound differentiation
    - ▪ Syllable segmentation
    - ▪ Sound blending and sound deletion.
    - ▪ Sound manipulation

Sounds and spelling patterns

There are 26 letters in the English alphabet that are used to represent between 42 and 44 sounds (depending on accent). These sounds are referred to as phonemes, and one change can give a completely different meaning to a word (*big pig*, or *hot hat*). Letters and letter combinations, also known as graphemes, represent the sounds on paper.

26 letters representing up 44 sounds is not a neat match; some letters represent more than one sound (*th, ow, oo*), and some sounds are represented by two or three letters (digraphs and trigraphs). The table below is not intended for learner use, but may be useful for instructors.

Common spelling patterns

	Common spelling	Spelling alternatives				
b	b: big	bb: rubber				
d	d: dig	dd: address	ed: called			
f	f: fun	ff: off	ph: photo	gh: cough	lf: half	ft: often
g	g: get	gg: egg	gh: Afghan	gu: guess	gue: fatigue	
h	h: hot	wh: whole				
dʒ	j: jar	ge: huge	g: giraffe	dge: edge	di: soldier	gg: bigger
k	k: key	c: cut	ch: school	cc: soccer	lk: yolk	qu: mosquito
		ck: back	x: six	q(u): quick		
l	l: lick	ll: smell				
m	m: money	mm: summer	mb: thumb	mn: autumn	lm: calm	
n	n: nose	nn: runner	kn: know	gn: sign	pn: pneumonia	
ŋ	ng: ring	n: sink	ngue: tongue			
p	p: pin	pp: apple				
r	r: red	rr: carry	wr: write	rh: rhyme		
s	s: sock	ss: dress	c: city	sc: science	ps psychology	st: listen
		se: horse	ce: cent			
t	t: top	tt: butter	th: thomas	ed: tapped	bt: debt:	

	Common spelling	Spelling alternatives				
v	v: vine	f: of	ph: Stephen	ve: five		
w	w: web	wh: when	u: quiet	o: choir		
j	y: yes					
z	z: zip	zz: puzzle	s: has	ss: scissors	x: xylophone	ze: breeze
		se: cheese				
ʒ	s: measure	si: vision	z: seizure			
tʃ	ch: chop	tch: match	tu: future	ti: action	te: righteous	
ʃ	sh: shop	ce: ocean	s: sugar	ci: facial	si: suspension	ch: machine
		sci: conscienc	ti: nation			
θ	th: thumb					
ð	th: father					
æ	a: hat	ai: plait				
ɛ	e: peg	ea: bread	u: bury	ie: friend	ai: said	a: many
ɪ	i: ink	e: pretty	o: women	u: busy	ui: building	y: gym
ɒ	o: orange	a: wash	ho: honest	ou: cough		
ʌ	u: mug	o: money	oo: blood	ou: touch		
ʊ	oo: look	u: pull	ou: should	o: wolf		
eɪ	ai: mail	a: table	eigh: eight	aigh: straight	ay: tray	
		ei: veil	au: gauge	a-e: lake	ea: break	ey: they

	Common spelling	Spelling alternatives				
i	ee: bee	e: me	ea: eat	y: happy	ey: key	oe: people
		ie: field	i: ski	ei: ceiling	eo: people	e_e: athlete
aɪ	i: find	y: sky	igh: light	ie: tie	uy: buy	i_e: bike
		ai: aisle	is: island	eigh: height		
oʊ	oa: soap	o-e: home	o: open	oe: toe	ow: slow	ough: dough
u	oo: soon	ew: screw	ue: blue	u_e: flute	oe: shoes	ough: through
		ui: fruit	o: who	ou: soup		
ju	u: uniform	you: you	ew: new	iew: view	u_e: cube	eau: beautiful
ɔɪ	oi: oil	oy: soy				
aʊ	ow: now	ou: house	ough: drought			
ə	er: sister	ar: collar	our: flavour	or: mirror	re: centre	
ɛə	air: hair	are: square	ear: tear	ere: there	eir: their	ayer: prayer
a	ar: car	a: father	au: aunt	er: sergeant	ear: heart	alm: calm
ɜ	ir: bird	er: herb	ur: surf	ear: heard	or: word	our: journey
ɔ	aw: draw	al: walk	or: cork	oor: door	ore: more	oar: board
		our: four	augh: taught	ar: war	ough: fought	au: august
ɪə	ear: ear	eer: deer	ere: here	ier: pier		
ʊə	ure: pure	our: tour				

Figure 30: Common spelling patterns

Word Bank

The vocabulary Word Bank has been drawn from the vocabulary used for life in Australia and has been specifically designed to list words that language learners are likely to know separately from those that are less likely to be known. These are listed as 'common' and 'rare'. The common words are more likely to be in learners' existing vocabulary or to be easy to give a relevant context for the word, while the rare words are less likely to be familiar to EALD learners.

This Word Bank is not intended as a resource for learners, but is a resource for instructors to use to develop class exercises and reading activities or to give examples of digraphs and sounds in class.

The 'tweakable' words are simply words have a spelling pattern that is not different enough to be considered irregular, but they do have alternate sounds or spelling patterns that will need attention from learners. For example, in the word *Kakadu*, the sounds *k a k a d* are regular, and only the letter *u* has an alternate sound.

Word Bank

\multicolumn{3}{Words with specific consonant-vowel patterns}		
vc	common	it, an, at, if, in, on, up, us
cvc	common	bad, bag, ban, bat, bed, beg, bet, bib, bid, big, bin, bit, box, bug, bum, bun, bus, but, can, cap, cat, cot, cup, cut, dad, dam, did, dig, dip, dob, dog, dot, dug, fan, fat, fed, fig, fin, fit, fix, fog, fox, fun, gap, gas, get, god, got, gum, gun, had, ham, hat, hen, hid, him, hip, hit, hop, hot, hug, jam, job, jog, jug, kid, lap, leg, let, lid, lip, lit, lot, mad, man, map, mat, max, men, met, mix, mop, mud, mug, mum, nod, not, nut, pad, pan, pat, peg, pen, pet, pig, pin, pip, pit, pot, pub, rag, ram, ran, rat, red, rib, rid, rip, rob, rub, rug, run, sad, sat, set, sex, sit, six, sum, sun, tag, tan, tap, tax, ten, tin, tip, top, tub, van, vet, wax, web, wet, win, wok, yes, yet, yuk, yum, zip
	rare	ben, bob, bop, bot, bub, bud, cob, cod, cog, com, dag, dan, deb, dim, doc, don, fib, gig, gus, gut, hem, hum, hut, jan, jen, jet, jim, keg, ken, kim, lab, lad, liz, log, mel, nan, nap, ned, net, nun, pam, pap, pav, pod, pop, rim, rod, ron, rot, rum, sam, sap, sip, ted, tim, tom, viv, wag, wig, yak, yam, yap, zit
vcc	common	add, and, ant, end, ink, its
	rare	act, elf, imp
ccvc	common	clap, clip, crab, drip, drop, drum, flag, flat, frog, from, glad, grab, gram, plan, plug, plum, plus, pram, prep, scan, skim, skin, skip, slap, slim, slip, slug, slum, smog, snap, spin, spit, spot, step, stop, swim, tram, trim, trip, twig, twin
	rare	brad, brag, bran, brim, clam, clot, club, cram, crib, croc, crop, drag, drug, flab, flan, flap, flip, fran, fred, fret, gran, greg, grid, grim, grin, grip, grit, grog, grot, grub, gwen, prom, scab, scam, scum, skid, slab, slam, slat, slid, slit, slob, slog, slop, slot, snip, spam, spat, stan, stem, stub, stud, stun, swam, swum, trap, trek, trot

Words with specific consonant-vowel patterns		
cvcc	**common**	bags, band, bank, belt, bend, bent, best, bond, bulk, bump, bunk, camp, cost, desk, disc, disk, dump, dust, fact, fast, fats, felt, film, fist, gift, gums, hand, help, hunt, jump, junk, just, lamp, land, left, lend, lift, list, lost, lots, mend, milk, mint, must, nest, next, nuts, pink, rent, rest, sand, sank, send, sent, sink, soft, tank, test, text, vest, wasp, went, west, wind,
	rare	bolt, bulb, bust, colt, conk, cult, damp, dank, dent, dunk, dusk, fink, font, gulf, gulp, held, hilt, hint, kelp, limp, link, lint, lump, lust, mask, mast, melt, mist, pant, pest, ramp, risk, rust, sift, silk, silt, sulk, sunk, tact, taft, tamp, task, temp, tent, tilt, tint, tusk, weld, wilt, wink, yank, yelp, zinc
vccv	**rare**	undo
vcvc	**rare**	Adam, edit, exam, exit
cvcvc	**common**	debit, denim, habit, japan, kebab, lemon, limit, login, melon, salad, seven, visit, vomit
	rare	camel, cumin, kevin, panic, petal, rapid, satin, sedan, tamil, topic, toxic, venom, wagon
vccvc	**common**	unfit, until, unzip, upset
	rare	album, atlas, enrol, expel, inbox, index
vcvcc	**common**	adult
	rare	adopt
ccvcc	**common**	blank, blend, blink, blond, blunt, crust, drank, drink, drunk, frost, grand, spend, spent, stamp, stand, stink, twins, twist
	rare	bland, brand, brink, clamp, clogs, cramp, crest, crisp, drift, flunk, frisk, gland, grant, grump, grunt, plank, plump, prank, print, skink, spank, spelt, studs, stump, swept, trend, trump, trunk, trust
cccvc	**common**	scrub, strap
	rare	scrap, splat, split, sprig, strip
cvccc	**common**	pants
	rare	mumps, pumps

Words with specific consonant-vowel patterns		
cvccvc	common	cobweb, helmet, hotdog, landed, laptop, nutmeg, petrol, picnic, public, rental, sunhat, sunset, suntan, wombat
	rare	banded, bedbug, cactus, candid, condom, fabric, velvet, victim
ccvcvc	common	clinic, credit, stupid, travel
	rare	brazil, planet, prison, profit, status, tripod, tropic
cvcvcc	common	result, second, tenant, vacant
cvcvcv	rare	mexico
vccvcc	common	absent
	rare	abduct, eldest, expand, expect, extend, impact, infant, infect, inject, insect, insist, insult, intend, invest, itself, unrest
cccvcc	common	strict
	rare	script, splint, sprint, strand, strips
ccvccc	rare	prompt

Double letters	off, Anna, back, bell, bill, boss, buff, buzz, dill, doll, duck, dull, fell, fill, full, gull, hill, kick, kill, kiss, less, lick, lock, luck, mess, Miss, neck, nick, null, pack, pick, pill, rock, roll, sell, sick, sock, suck, tell, tick, well, will, yell, yuck, added, asset, black, block, brick, click, cliff, clock, comma, crack, cross, dress, drill, flick, floss, frill, grill, hello, scull, skull, smack, smell, snack, socks, spell, spill, stick, still, stuck, track, troll, across, addict, assess, assets, assist, attack, attend, banned, billed, bitten, bogged, bonnet, bottom, bucket, button, canned, cannot, capped, carrot, common, cotton, docket, enroll, funnel, happen, hiccup, hidden, jacket, kitten, lesson, locked, missed, muffin, packed, packet, pocket, possum, punnet, rabbit, ribbon, ripped, scroll, scruff, stress, struck, sudden, ticket, address, antenna, attempt, attract, blossom, cassava, clapped, classic, cockpit, collect, command, comment, connect, cricket, cropped, discuss, dismiss, dropped, eggroll, express, fattest, fitness, flannel, glasses, paddock, padlock, pickled, traffic, appendix, assisted, backpack, bandanna, brussels, buttocks, crockpot, dandruff, eggplant, enrolled, espresso, freckles, lipstick, prickles, assistant, attendant, connected, depressed, difficult, drumstick, immigrant, rockmelon, assessment, commitment, controlled, disconnect, pickpocket
Tweakable words	ago, emu, flu, son, uni, acne, deli, kilo, last, pass, past, raft, sofa, taxi, tofu, tuna, visa, yolk, ankle, apple, bacon, basil, begin, class, comma, craft, folic, front, gecko, glass, grass, hello, humid, Islam, isn't, litre, metre, music, pasta, pilot, pizza, plant, rhino, rinse, staff, taste, uncle, waste, woman, zebra, banana, basket, battle, bikini, bubble, buckle, candle, cattle, cuddle, demand, Kakadu, kettle, lesson, litres, metres, middle, muslim, pimple, potato, puddle, puzzle, rattle, refund, secret, simple, single, tahini, tangle, tomato, tunnel, twelve, vacuum, avocado, classes, coconut, crumble, diploma, drizzle, expense, glasses, grandma, grandpa, grumble, migrant, minibus, pretend, prevent, program, sultana, tobacco, vanilla, vitamin, volcano, assemble, broccoli, eggplant, freckles, grandson, horrible, occupant, omelette, prickles, scramble, scribble, sensible, sultanas, terrible, umbrella, spaghetti, antiseptic, impossible, incredible, millilitre, millilitres, responsible, conjunctivitis

Words with specific digraphs or letters		
ch	**common**	bench, benchtop, branch, bunch, chat, check, check-up, chef, chest, chestnut, chicken, child, children, chili, chilli, chin, china, chips, chop, chopsticks, church, french, lunch, lunchbox, much, rich, spinach
	rare	attach, avalanche, belch, chalk, channel, chant, chapati, chess, chickenpox, grandchild, grandchildren, pinch, punch, stench, step-child, step-children, such, kitchen, kitchenhand
y	**common**	yak, yams, yank, yell, yes, yet, yuck, yum
	rare	yakka, yolk, yoga, yogi, kenyan
sh	**common**	brush, bush, cash, crash, dishes, eggshell, finish, fish, push, rubbish, rush, she, shed, she'd, shelf, shell, she'll, she's, shift, ship, shop, shut, wash
	rare	ash, ashes, astonish, bishop, blush, british, crush, Danish, dash, dish, fishnet, fishpond, flesh, fresh, furnish, mash, nutshell, polish, punish, radish, rash, selfish, shallots, shellfish, shelves, shin, shock, shot, shred, shrimp, shrink, shrub, shrug, shrunk, shuffle, spanish, splash, Swedish, trash, turkish, unfinished, vanish, washable, welsh, wish, yiddish
ai	**common**	mail, mailbox, main, paid, pain, rain, train, wait
	rare	ukrainian, afraid, again, against, aid, aim, aimless, available, bail, bait, bandaid, braid, brain, claim, cocktail, complain, contain, curtain, details, drain, explain, fail, faint, gain, grain, hail, handrail, hotmail, jail, laid, maid, maintain, multigrain, nail, obtain, painful, painless, paint, paintbox, pigtails, plain, postpaid, prepaid, raid, rail, rainfall, raisin, regain, remain, retail, sail, snail, Spain, sprain, stain, tail, trail, unafraid, unpaid, waist, waitress
oa	**common**	boat, coat, loan, road, soap, toast
	rare	croatian, bloat, boast, cloak, coast, crossroad, float, foam, goal, goat, groan, hoax, load, loaf, moan, oats, paddleboat, roast, soak, toad, unload
ie	**common**	die, died, lie, lied, pie, tie, tied, fried, magpie, tried
	rare	pied, cried, diet, dried, piecrust, client, applied, denied, untie, necktie, replied, modified, satisfied, dissatisfied

		Words with specific digraphs or letters
ee	common	asleep, bee, beef, been, beep, bleed, canteen, coffee, deep, feel, feet, fifteen, free, green, meet, need, peel, screen, see, sixteen, sleep, street, sunscreen, sweep, sweet, tree, week
	rare	agree, beeswax, beet, beetle, between, committee, creek, creep, degree, disagree, fee, feed, flatscreen, flee, freedom, Frisbee, greed, greek, greenland, greet, gumtree, heel, jeep, keep, leek, mallee, midweek, needle, needs, reef, seed, seem, seen, self-esteem, speed, speedos, spleen, steel, steep, steeple, teen, toffee, toll-free, treefrog, treetop, wee, weed, weep, weevil
or	common	or, born, cord, corn, for, fork, form, horn, pork, port, sport, storm, supports, important, passport, uniform
	rare	organic, cork, organ, hormonal, ford, fort, horse, sort, torn, worn, york, formal, normal, portable, cordial, formula, forklift, format, snort, snorkel, support, acorn, deport, import, inform, informal, record, report, Victoria, export, landlord, popcorn, unaffordable, corridor, platform, duststorm, sandstorm, transport, unicorn, osteoporosis
oo	common	book, cook, foot, good, look, wood, wool, spoonful, classroom, kookaburra
	rare	hood, hook, took, booklet, cookbook, football, footprint, footstep, stood, woollen, unhook, handbook, restroom, stockroom, driftwood, textbook
oo	common	broom, boot, cool, food, moon, roof, room, soon, too, zoo, Google, spoon, bedroom
	rare	groom, broomstick, boost, hoof, loo, loop, mood, noon, pool, roo, root, tool, bloom, noodles, poodle, proof, scoop, stool, troops, baboon, balloon, igloo, lagoon, tattoo, monsoon, bandicoot, cockatoo, tablespoon, toolbox

		Words with specific digraphs or letters
ng	**common**	asking, baking, biting, bring, calling, coming, driving, dropping, ending, fasting, helping, listening, living, long, making, ring, sing, sitting, smoking, song, spelling, spring, standing, stepping, sting, stockings, stopping, string, strong, swimming, taking, texting, visiting, vomiting, voting, walking, waving, wedding, wing, winning
	rare	along, amazing, bang, banking, becoming, belong, bending, betting, bettong, biking, billabong, billing, braking, burning, camping, clapping, clicking, cling, closing, collecting, communicating, competing, completing, computing, confusing, coping, costing, cracking, craving, crippling, crossing, curling, cutting, dating, disgusting, diving, drink-driving, drinking, during, enrolling, estimating, examining, expecting, filling, fitting, grilling, grinning, hang, having, hunting, including, incoming, jumping, kicking, king, landing, locking, losing, lung, melting, missing, mixing, moving, nodding, non-smoking, nursing, packing, paving, planning, planting, posting, printing, resting, ripping, rising, running, saving, savings, sending, siblings, skating, skiing, skipping, slang, sliding, sling, slipping, smiling, sniffing, spitting, stinking, stung, sung, surfing, surprising, swelling, swing, tangle, tasting, testing, timing, tipping, translating, unpacking, using, zoning
th **ð**	**common**	than, that, that'd, that's, them, then, this, clothes, with
	rare	bedclothes, furthest, sunbathe, themselves, withheld, within
th **θ**	**common**	bath, bathtub, both, cloth, mathematics, maths, moth, month, path, sixth, tenth, thank, thanks, thanked, thick, thin, think
	rare	anthem, athletic, athletics, bandwidth, depth, ethnic, fifth, hundredth, catholic, cathedral, locksmith, mothball, method, smith, tablecloth, truth, width, thankful, theft, thicken, throb
qu	**common**	equal, quick, quilt, quit, request
	rare	aquatic, equipment, frequent, kumquat, liquid, quack, quandong, quicksand, quiz, quokka, quoll, quota, quran, squid, squint

		Words with specific digraphs or letters	
ou	**common**	about, loud, cloud, flour, out	
	rare	account, accountant, amount, blackout, campground, cloudless, count, deposit account, discount, doubt, dropout, found, ground, grout, handout, aloud, noun, outback, outbid, outcast, pronoun, recount, round, scout, sound, sprout, sprouts, surround, ultrasound, walkout	
oi	**common**	boil, coin, oil	
	rare	android, appointment, avoid, ballpoint, coil, disappointed, foil, hoist, join, joint, moist, oilcan, ointment, point, poison, soil, spoil, spoilt, tinfoil, topsoil	
ue	**common**	blue, glue	
	rare	clue, cue, due, issue, tissue, untrue, value, venue, fondue, rescue, statue, continue, fluent, gluestick	
er	**common**	her, herb, herd, hers, herself, persian, perfect, person, bermuda, internet, pepper, peppermint, transfer	
	rare	persimmon, fern, jerk, kerb, nerd, nerves, perm, serb, serve, served, term, verb, dermatitis, herbal, pergola, servant, serbian, vertical, vertigo, vertebra, ferment, hermit, kernel, permit, personal, terminal, sternum, internal, interpret, converter, convert, expert, external, midterm, perhaps, persist, terrific, verandah, insert, interrupt, pattern, patterned	
er	**common**	better, butter, dinner, enter, ladder, letter, letterbox, litter, rubber, runner, summer, under, understand, after, answer, jumper, sister, winter	
	rare	poster, offer, otter, upper, batter, biller, bitter, colander, copper, cutter, fatter, gutters, hammer, heron, hotter, killer, locker, manners, matter, packer, robber, spanner, sadder, salamander, sclerosis, seller, simmer, sitter, stroller, teller, winner, bladder, bumper, busker, caller, cracker, dropper, drummer, duster, fender, filter, flippers, foster, fritter, glitter, helper, renter, scanner, silver, softer, spinner, stammer, sticker, swimmer, tanker, temper, tender, toddler, welder, blender, blister, faster, printer, smaller, stapler, backpacker, disaster, sprinkler, helicopter, midwinter, nutcracker, stepladder, gallbladder, half-sister, step-sister, dobber, rubberband	

		Words with specific digraphs or letters
ar	**common**	arm, bar, bark, car, card, dark, far, farm, hard, jar, mark, park, part, garden, garlic, market, parsnip, scarf, scarves, smart, star, start, alarm, apart, apartment, started, Antarctic, depart, rhubarb
	rare	armed, armenian, art, Arctic, armadillo, armpit, armrest, arson, article, artist, barn, carp, cart, dart, harm, harp, lard, Mars, marsupial, tar, tart, yard, yarn, barnacle, carbon, cardamom, cardiac, cardigan, carpet, carsick, carton, darkest, Darwin, gargle, garment, harden, harmful, harmless, harness, harvest, marble, martial, marzipan, pardon, parka, parmesan, scar, spark, starve, tartan, scarlet, smartest, sparkle, department, regard, Antarctica, mascara, sandbar, handlebars, postcard, postmark, leotard, altar, barista, barracuda, barramundi, cardamon, Hobart
a_e	**common**	ate, bake, brake, cake, date, game, gave, grape, hate, immigrate, lake, lane, late, lemonade, made, make, make-up, male, mane, mate, mistake, name, pale, plane, plate, rates, sale, same, save, snake, state, take, translate, update, wake, wave
	rare	academic, accommodate, accurate, activate, advocate, amaze, animated, approximate, base, baseball, became, behave, blade, blame, blaze, calculate, came, candidate, cane, cape, case, cave, climate, communicate, complicated, confiscate, consulate, crane, crate, cupcake, database, decade, delicate, demonstrate, dictate, discriminate, donate, educated, emigrate, escape, estimate, fade, fake, female, flake, flame, flatmate, folate, frame, frustrated, gate, grade, grave, graze, hake, handbrake, hazelnut, inhale, insane, intake, jade, locate, maze, medicated, meditate, migrate, misbehave, naked, pancake, private, rebate, related, relocate, safe, scales, scrape, sedate, senate, skate, slave, spade, stake, stale, sunbake, tape, trade
e_e	**rare**	compete, complete, concrete, delete, discrete, eve, even, event, extreme, incomplete, maltese, Pete, severe, supreme

Words with specific digraphs or letters		
i_e	common	bedtime, bike, bite, crime, crocodile, describe, dive, drive, drive-in, expensive, file, fine, five, full-time, hide, jobactive, like, lime, line, mine, mobile, nine, pipe, ride, size, slide, smile, spine, sunrise, surprise, time, wife
	challenging	active, additive, adhesive, adjective, advise, aggressive, alike, alive, appetite, attractive, bagpipes, beside, bile, bite-sized, bribe, bride, brine, business, captive, clockwise, compromise, confident, cursive, define, destructive, dislike, disruptive, divide, examine, ex-wife, frostbite, hike, hive, hotline, immunised, impolite, inactive, intestines, invite, kite, life, midwife, neckline, nile, pile, pine, pipeline, polite, prescribe, prize, reptile, ripe, rise, risen, rockslide, saline, sedatives, sensitive, side, slime, spike, stripe, tide, tile, timetable, tribe, tripe, unripe, vine, website, wide, wildlife, wine, wipe
o_e	common	bone, broke, close, coke, gloves, home, note, postcode, smoke, stove, vote, woke, zone
	challenging	alone, antelope, antidote, backbone, backstroke, clove, cone, cope, cove, dole, dome, dose, doze, drove, explode, flagpole, froze, frozen, gallstones, globe, glovebox, homesick, hope, hose, joke, nose, pope, rode, rome, rope, rose, spoke, stole, stolen, stone, stroke, sunstroke, tadpole, t-bone, token, tote
u_e	common	confused, culture, cure, excuse, furniture, fuse, future, include, June, picture
	challenging	abuse, accuse, acupuncture, agriculture, altitude, assume, attitude, bitumen, capsule, commute, costume, cube, cured, cute, dentures, disclosure, dispute, document, dune, exclude, figure, flute, focused, fracture, fractured, fumes, immature, immune, injure, insecure, institute, instrument, insure, lecture, legume, manure, mature, minute, mixture, mule, mute, nature, Neptune, nude, pedicure, pollute, posture, premature, pressure, prune, puncture, pure, refuse, rubella, rude, rule, salute, secure, substitute, tube, tune, unused, use, used, useful, ute, volume, vulture

		Words with specific digraphs or letters
y	**common**	baby, crazy, lazy, ladybug, copy, lucky, sticky, daddy, muddy, teddy, badly, fluffy, stuffy, fifty, foggy, ugly, tidy, untidy, activity, disability, eligibility, belly, jelly, lolly, mummy, grumpy, tenancy, vacancy, kindy, windy, funny, skinny, sunny, plenty, twenty, body, happy, nappy, puppy, unhappy, empty, esky, messy, dusty, softly, strictly, entry, pantry, pastry, jetty, study, skivvy, sixty, dizzy, frizzy, fuzzy
	challenging	navy, wavy, bubbly, possibly, probably, bilby, lacy, rocky, swampy, reluctantly, piggyback, democracy, rugby, oxygen, baggy, bumpy, lumpy, nasty, tasty, gently, mostly, promptly
ay	**common**	day, may, pay, say, way, play, playful, spray, today, friday, Monday, prepay, sunday, rent payment
	challenging	pay back, pay bill, pay slip, bay, hay, jay, lay, payable, payday, payment, ray, ways, gay, play mat, play pen, stay slim, abaya, bpay, clay, crayon, gray, okay, playpen, pray, stay, tray, delay, essay, relay, repayment, stray, x-ray, decay, midday, replay, runway, subway, sunray, display, holiday, bugspray, spillway, Anzac Day, Crisis Payment, expressway, tap and pay, public holiday
oy	**common**	boy, toy
	challenging	soy milk, toy box, boycott, joyful, joystick, soy, annoy, enjoy, enjoyable, convoy, employ, employment, destroy, soft toy, stuffed toy
ea	**common**	beancurd, beans, clean, cream, east, eat, heat, jeans, leak, meat, peanut, peas, read, real, scream, sea, seat, seatbelt, speak, tea, teabag, teacup, teapot
	challenging	appeal, bead, beagle, beak, beam, beat, bedspread, deal, dream, eagle, feast, flea, heal, heap, lead, leaf, leaflet, lean, leap, leapfrog, least, meal, mean, means, measles, meatball, mislead, misread, neat, peacock, peak, reason, seagrass, seagull, seal, sealant, seam, seasick, season, seasonal, steal, steam, stream, team, treat, treatment, unclean, weak, wean, yeast, zealand
y	**common**	apply, by, dry, fly, fry, frypan, my, notify, occupy, rye, sky, standby, try, cry, butterfly
	challenging	bicycle, cycle, reply, dragonfly, deny, cypress

Words with specific digraphs or letters		
ow - oa	**common**	own, low, low-cost, grow, slow, snow, elbow, pillow, widow, yellow, mow
	challenging	owe, bowl, row, sow, tow, tow truck, rowed, blow, crow, flow, glow, lowest, arrow, below, disown, follow, hollow, willow, swallow, crossbow
ow - ou	**common**	cow, down, how, now, brow, brown, crowd, frown, towel, towel rack, vowel, allow
	challenging	owl, bow, howl, town, vow, clown, crown, downhill, drown, growl, plow, scowl, crowded, trowel, sundown, Townsville
ir	**common**	bird, confirm, dirt, firm, first, miniskirt, skirt, stir, girl, sir
	challenging	fir, flirt, spiral
ew	**common**	new, news
	challenging	andrew, blew, brew, crew, crewcut, dew, drew, few, flew, grew, hebrew, Jew, mildew, Newcastle, pew, screw, stew, unscrew
ur	**common**	burn, burned, burnt, burp, fur, hurt, nurse, purple, purse, return, suburb, sunburn, sunburnt, surf, turn, yoghurt
	challenging	burnoff, burqini, burst, curve, kurd, lemur, nocturnal, saturn, disturb
igh	**common**	bright, fight, flight, fright, frighten, high, light, lights, midnight, night, right, rights, sight, sunlight, tight, tighten, tights, tonight
	challenging	alright, brightness, candlelight, highest, highjack, highland, highlight, lighten, lightest, might, nightdress, nightfall, nightlight, nightstand, sigh, skintight, slight, spotlight, twilight
wh	**common**	what, when
	challenging	whip, whisk, whistle, whizzes
aw	**common**	crawl, draw, jaw, jigsaw, law, raw, saw, yawn
	challenging	awful, brawl, claw, dawn, fawn, hacksaw, handsaw, hawk, in-law, lawn, macaw, paw, prawn, son-in-law, straw
au	**common**	August, laundromat
	challenging	applaud, astronaut, auto, automatic, caustic, dinosaur, exhaust, exhausted, fraud, glaucoma, haul, haunt, haunted, trauma, traumatic, pause

Words with specific digraphs or letters		
ph	**common**	photo, photograph
	challenging	apostrophe, asphalt, catastrophe, dolphin, emphasis, esophagus, graph, pamphlet, prophet, saxophonist, sphinx
old	**common**	old, gold, sold, hold, told, fold, cold, golden
	challenging	bold, mold, unfold, behold, holden, manifold, oldest, scold, goldenrod, handhold, tenfold, unfolded, unmold
al	**common**	all, ball, basketball, call, called, fall, hall, mall, netball, small, smallest, talk, tall, walk, wall, walnut
	challenging	fallen, gumball, install, recall, smallpox, softball
ies	**common**	babies, cries, curries, dies, difficulties, disabilities, dries, dummies, families, flies, fries, ladies, lies, lollies, luckiest, messiest, movies, nappies, notifies, penalties
	challenging	abilities, activities, bodies, communities, companies, copies, pokies, puppies, responsibilities, skies, studies, tries
ce	**common**	absence, accent, accept, assistance, attendance, cancel, cell, census, cent, centre, centrelink, dance, danced, distance, entrance, excel, excellent, fence, france, mince, minced, offence, once, recommence, romance, scent, sentence, since, success, successful
	challenging	abscess, acceptable, acceptance, access, accessible, advance, advanced, commence, concept, convince, essence, except, finance, finances, prince, princess, scenic, substance, unacceptable
ci	**common**	decimal, principal, antacid, cicada, cinnamon, pacific, pencil, racism, racist, appendicitis, circle
	challenging	acid, acidic, citrus, rancid, specific, stencil, disciple, criticism
ge	**common**	gem, suggest, gentle, gentleman
	challenging	analgesic, gel, gelatin, genitals, gent
gi	**common**	begin, digital, ginger
	challenging	magic, tragic, eligible, giggle, illegible, legible
dg	**common**	bridge, bridging, budget, budgie, edge, fridge, judge
	challenging	judgment, badge, fidget, fudge, hedge, ledge, lodge, lodgement, nudge, ridge, sledge, smudge, trudge, wedge

Words with specific digraphs or letters		
wr	common	wrap, wrist
	challenging	wraps, wreck, wren, wrestle, wriggle, written
kn	common	knit, knitted, knob, knock, knocked, knot, knuckle
	challenging	knapsack
or - er	common	word, work, world, worm
	challenging	worse, worst, silkworm
air	common	air, airbag, aircraft, Cairns, fair, hair, hairband, haircut, pair, repair, stairs, unfair, upstairs
	challenging	airlift, despair
ear	common	beard, clear, dear, disappear, ear, eardrop, earn, fear, hear, near, rear, rear-end, tear, year
	challenging	appear, earwig, fear, smear, eardrum

Add or Delete One Sound

Initial sound	Final sound
age - cage	be - beach
air - chair	be - bean
all - call	bell - belt
and - sand	bow - boat
ants - pants	by - bike
ape - tape	by - bite
arm - farm	car - card
art - part	car - cart
ask - task	day - date
at - hat	far - farm
ate - bait	he - heap
ate - gate	he - heat
ate - late	lay - late
ate- gate	lay - late
cake - ache	lie - light
car - scar	live - liver
eat - meat	low - load
eat - seat	may - make
I - my	me - meat
ice - rice	my - mice
in - shin	no - nose
itch - which	no - note
lay - play	pay - page
lean - clean	pit - pita
lick - click	row - road
lip - slip	see -seat
live - olive	she - sheep
no - snow	so - soak
pain - paint	star - start
pit - spit	sun - sunny
row - grow	tie - tide
rub - scrub	way - weight
tea - team	we - weed
top - stop	why - white

Compound Words

into	seasick	seatbelt	peppermint
onto	seaweed	soysauce	pillowcase
inside	stepson	suitcase	playground
nearby	sunburn	takeaway	secondhand
peanut	sunrise	teenager	skateboard
sunset	toenail	textbook	stepfather
teapot	weekend	bookshelf	stepmother
airport	backpack	childcare	stepsister
ashtray	backward	chopsticks	strawberry
barcode	backyard	classmate	sunglasses
bedroom	bathroom	classroom	tablecloth
carsick	birthday	classwork	toothbrush
daytime	blackout	dragonfly	toothpaste
desktop	cupboard	drainpipe	watermelon
doormat	daydream	everybody	waterproof
doorway	daylight	grapevine	wheelchair
dustpan	doorbell	handshake	windowsill
earlobe	driveway	headphones	breadcrumbs
eyebrow	eggplant	highchair	grandfather
eyelash	eggshell	nosebleed	grandmother
grandma	football	photocopy	grandparent
grandpa	grandson	surfboard	hairdresser
haircut	handmade	babysitter	handwriting
halfway	hayfever	childbirth	righthanded
hallway	headache	dishwasher	screwdriver
handbag	homemade	earthquake	stepbrother
handout	homesick	fingernail	supermarket
highway	homework	grandchild	underweight
lookout	keyboard	grapefruit	wheelbarrow
outside	landlord	highschool	blackberries
overdue	overseas	lefthanded	cheeseburger
popcorn	passport	motorcycle	stepdaughter
railway	password	newsletter	thunderstorm
rainbow	raincoat	nightshift	grandchildren
seafood	saucepan	outpatient	granddaughter

Minimal triplets

a	e	i	o	u
an		in	on	
bad	bed	bid		bud
bag	beg	big		bug
bait	beat	bite	boat	boot
ball	bell	bill		bull
band	bend		bond	
bat	bet	bit		but
cat			cot	cut
drag	dreg			drug
fan		fin		fun
far			for	fur
fast		fist	fort	
hack	heck	hick	hock	
ham	hem	him		hum
hat		hit	hot	hut
last		list	lost	lust
mash	mesh		mosh	mush
mass	mess	miss	moss	
mast		mist	most	must
mate		mite		mute
pack	peck	pick		
pale		pile	pole	
pan	pen	pin		pun
pat	pet	pit	pot	put
rack		rick	rock	ruck
ram		rim		rum
rat			rot	rut
sat	set	sit		
slat		slit	slot	
tan	ten	tin		
	get		got	gut
	let	lit	lot	
	net	nit	not	nut
		pip	pop	pup

Rhymes

Rhymes	
ab	nab, slab, stab, cab, jab, crab, blab, lab, scab, tab, grab, flab, dab, drab
able	able, gable, stable, table, fable, sable, cable
ace	ace, brace, mace, place, grace, race, lace, pace, face, space, trace
ack	yak, back, rack, hack, tack, lack, pack, slack, whack, sack, smack, black, snack, stack, crack, track, knack, quack, flack, shack, clack, attack, Jack, Zack
act	act, tract, fact, pact, subtract
ad	bad, glad, brad, tad, had, pad, clad, fad, doodad, mad, Dad, sad, cad, lad
ade	made, jade, grade, shade, blade, wade, glade, fade, spade
ag	bag, flag, wag, stag, drag, lag, snag, hag, sag, swag, crag, rag, nag, gag, brag, tag
age	age, page, sage, cage, engage, rage, wage, stage
aid	aid, paid, laid, maid, raid, braid
ail	ail, tail, flail, rail, fail, hail, trail, sail, bail, tale, nail, ale, hale, kale, gale, stale, male, snail, frail, dale, quail, pail, detail, jail, avail, email, mail, bale, whale, wail, pale, sale, scale, shale
ain	sprain, chain, Spain, vain, pain, drain, complain, stain, grain, explain, lain, obtain, main, rain, strain, train, gain, brain, plain, slain
air	aware, air, care, scare, stare, fair, spare, prepare, hair, bare, where, compare, declare, pare, glare, mare, swear, despair, beware, snare, flare, dare, square, bear, lair, ware, pair, pear, fairy, chair, there, flair, share, stair, rare, unfair, fare, hare, wear, repair
ait	eight, bait, gate, late, trait, gait, crate, slate, plate, ate, create, rate, debate, freight, fate, skate, mate, strait, wait, Kate, date, straight, grate, hate, sate, great, state, abate, relate, weight
ake	fake, brake, wake, flake, ache, make, shake, break, cake, snake, drake, awake, lake, quake, take, mistake, Jake, sake, rake, steak, bake, stake
alf	calf, half
alk	balk, walk, chalk, talk, stalk

Rhymes	
all	sprawl, all, gall, stall, squall, call, hall, crawl, small, football, enthrall, brawl, install, fall, pall, tall, thrall, baseball, mall, ball, wall, drawl, bawl, shawl
alm	balm, psalm, palm, calm
am	scam, gram, Sam, cam, dam, cram, tram, clam, lam, am, ma'am, sham, tam, ham, scram, yam, ram, Pam, jam, exam, swam, wham, slam, pram, dram, spam
ame	came, flame, game, same, blame, name, fame, lame, dame, tame, frame, shame
amp	camp, ramp, clamp, champ, cramp, lamp, tramp, damp, scamp, stamp
an	ran, fan, flan, an, began, tan, van, Fran, Stan, scan, pan, clan, can, man, ban, plan, Japan, Jan, pecan, bran, than, span, Dan
ance	dance, stance, trance, prance, glance, France, lance, chance
anch	ranch, branch
and	band, and, bland, sand, command, stand, grand, gland, land, demand, expand, understand, strand, hand
ane	cane, mane, vane, crane, sane, lane, pane, bane, wane
ang	bang, clang, hang, sang, slang, rang, gang, pang, fang, tang, twang, sprang
ange	range, strange, change, mange
ank	bank, dank, clank, shrank, lank, thank, Hank, blank, prank, yank, flank, drank, spank, shank, frank, tank, rank, crank, plank, sank
ant	pant, grant, slant, scant, plant, chant
ap	tap, trap, chap, nap, gap, scrap, zap, yap, slap, snap, wrap, cap, lap, map, flap, sap, rap, clap, strap
ape	ape, nape, grape, shape, drape, gape, tape, cape, scrape
ar	car, are, mar, spar, star, afar, scar, bar, tsar, far, jar, czar, guitar, tar, par
ard	card, lard, hard
arge	large, barge, charge
ark	ark, hark, park, shark, mark, dark, lark, bark, spark, stark
arm	arm, charm, harm, farm
arrow	arrow, marrow, barrow, harrow, narrow, sparrow
art	art, part, chart, start, dart, tart, cart
ash	smash, gash, flash, crash, ash, brash, lash, slash, dash, rash, mash, gnash, hash, cash, clash, splash, stash, thrash, bash, trash, sash
ask	ask, mask, cask, bask, task, flask
ass	grass, class, brass, glass

Rhymes	
ast	cast, past, fast, mast, last, blast
at	cat, chat, mat, rat, pat, bat, flat, slat, spat, vat, splat, sat, fat, hat, combat, that, brat, scat, at
atch	batch, latch, snatch, patch, hatch, match, catch, scratch
ave	cave, brave, rave, slave, crave, wave, pave, save, gave, stave, grave, shave
aw	saw, straw, slaw, jaw, law, claw, paw, draw, gnaw, caw, raw, thaw, flaw
awn	dawn, drawn, lawn, yawn, prawn
ax	lax, flax, wax, tax
ay	display, fray, play, way, may, stay, sway, bray, gay, away, spray, flay, nay, okay, quay, relay, they, ray, slay, hay, stray, grey, bay, lay, obey, pay, say, replay, pray, decay, tray, today, delay, day, clay, jay, gray
aze	daze, maze, faze, haze, graze, craze
ea	sea, tea, flea
each	beach, teach, peach, reach, bleach, preach
ead	dead, instead, read, shed, steady, dread, red, fled, tread, wed, bled, lead, bred, bread, fed, head, bed, spread, thread, ready, led, said, Ted
ead	bead, plead, read, lead
eak	beak, creak, teak, sneak, freak, bleak, peak, weak, leak, speak, squeak, streak
eal	deal, real, zeal, veal, peal, seal, meal, steal
eam	beam, team, cream, stream, steam, seam, gleam, ream, dream, scream
ean	bean, clean, mean, lean
eap	heap, cheap, reap, leap
ear(eer)	ear, year, gear, rear, clear, near, fear, hear, dear, tear, spear, shear
earn	earn, learn, yearn
east	beast, yeast, least, feast
eat	beat, cheat, wheat, seat, cleat, neat, meat, feat, beet, treat, heat, feet, fleet, eat, meet, greet, pleat, bleat, peat, sheet, sleet, street, sweet, tweet
eck	deck, fleck, neck, peck, speck, check
edge	edge, hedge, ledge, sledge, fledge, wedge, pledge
ee	bee, tee, flee, three, glee, see, wee, fee, free, tree
eech	leech, speech
eed	deed, breed, greed, creed, heed, need, seed, weed, speed, steed, tweed, reed, feed, bleed, freed
eek	meek, seek, creek, sleek, reek, week, peek, Greek
eel	wheel, eel, feel, peel, kneel, reel, steel, keel, heel

Rhymes	
een	keen, green, seen, been, screen, queen
eep	beep, steep, keep, peep, sheep, seep, creep, jeep, deep, sleep, sweep, weep
eer	beer, leer, sneer, cheer, steer, jeer, peer, deer, queer
eft	left, theft, bereft
eg	beg, leg, keg, peg
eigh	weigh, neigh, sleigh
eld	held, weld
elf	elf, shelf, self
ell	bell, motel, hotel, tell, jell, well, cell, farewell, smell, spell, fell, dell, swell, dwell, hell, sell, yell, shell
elp	help, yelp
em	hem, them, stem
en	den, again, fen, gentlemen, pen, then, open, Ben, amen, ten, glen, yen, men, hen, Gwen, children, Ken, when, wren
ench	bench, French, clench, drench, trench
end	bend, wend, mend, tend, blend, send, lend, rend, fend, vend, spend
ent	bent, accent, cent, tent, event, gent, sent, dent, went, lent, pent, rent, scent, vent, spent
ept	kept, swept, wept, slept, crept
esh	mesh, flesh, fresh
ess	mess, dress, less, bless, press, chess
est	best, chest, nest, zest, guest, test, jest, crest, pest, vest, west, rest, unrest, quest
et	bet, threat, let, upset, yet, jet, met, get, barrette, set, vet, pet, reset, fret, net, wet
etch	fetch, sketch, stretch
ew	crew, brew, drew, strew, slew, flew, screw, few, grew, dew, blew, renew, hew, mew, new, threw, knew, chew, pew, spew, stew
ext	next, text
ib	bib, nib, crib, glib, jib, rib, fib
ice	nice, ice, twice, price, rice, spice, dice, lice, mice, slice, splice, thrice, vice
ick	kick, thick, chick, trick, nick, wick, slick, lick, tick, flick, stick, sick, pick, Rick, quick, click, brick
id	slid, skid, kid, grid, lid, did, hid, bid, rid
ide	ride, bride, side, glide, pride, wide, hide, tide, bide, slide, stride
idge	ridge, porridge, fridge, bridge
ie	pie, die, lie, tie
ief	chief, thief, brief

Rhymes	
ife	fife, knife, wife, life, strife
iff	tiff, cliff, stiff, sniff
ift	gift, swift, lift, sift, shift
ig	big, dig, twig, fig, jig, sprig, swig, pig, rig, brig, wig
igh	high, nigh, sigh, thigh
ike	bike, spike, dike, like, hike, strike, pike
ild	mild, wild, child
ile	Nile, file, stile, while, pile, bile, mile, rile, smile, tile, vile
ilk	milk, silk
ill	pill, fill, till, hill, kill, will, sill, still, chill, thrill, Jill, frill, krill, spill, shrill, mill, gill, drill, trill, swill, quill, ill, grill, skill, bill, dill
ilt	hilt, tilt, wilt
im	dim, skim, him, grim, rim, vim, trim, prim, brim, slim, Jim, Tim, Kim, swim
ime	time, prime, lime, mime, slime, grime, crime
imp	limp, blimp, crimp, chimp
in	twin, bin, sin, din, win, fin, kin, spin, skin, tin, grin, gin, within, chin, shin, thin, begin, pin, in
ince	mince, since, wince, prince, quince
inch	finch, pinch, flinch
ind(ie)	bind, rind, find, grind, hind, kind, behind, blind, mind
ine	dine, pine, fine, line, vine, define, twine, swine, shrine, sine, brine, decline, shine, mine, wine, nine, spine, tine, whine
ing	string, sing, sling, wing, cling, bring, ping, swing, thing, sting, wring, spring, king, ring, fling, zing
inge	binge, hinge, singe, cringe, fringe
ink	sink, wink, mink, clink, slink, brink, rink, fink, ink, chink, link, drink, pink, shrink, stink, blink, think
int	dint, flint, lint, mint, tint, glint
ip	skip, slip, strip, ship, flip, clip, snip, quip, blip, chip, nip, rip, sip, tip, lip, whip, zip, dip, hip, drip, grip, trip
ipe	ripe, tripe, pipe, wipe, snipe, stripe, swipe
ir	fir, sir, stir
ird	bird, gird, third
ire	umpire, fire, inquire, wire, entire, tire, spire, desire, admire, inspire, retire, shire, aspire
irst	first, thirst
irt	dirt, flirt, skirt, shirt
ise	realise, comprise, supervise, surprise, surmise, sunrise, despise, advertise, chastise, exercise, enterprise, advise, apologise, recognise, mesmerise, economise, tranquilise, authorise, hypnotise, rise, wise, prise, sympathise, tantalise, dramatise, demise, baptise, memorise, utilise, organise

Rhymes	
ish	fish, wish, dish, swish
isk	disk, brisk, frisk
isp	lisp, crisp
iss	miss, hiss, kiss, bliss
ist	fist, list, mist, twist, grist
it	bit, skit, flit, nit, pit, slit, lit, split, admit, snit, spit, quit, grit, fit, sit, hit, commit, wit, permit, mit, it, knit, twit
itch	ditch, stitch, hitch, twitch, pitch, witch, which, rich, switch, snitch
ite	bite, kite, fight, site, white, fright, bright, write, flight, knight, might, night, plight, right, sight, slight, tonight, tight, height, light, delight, blight
ive	dive, drive, five, thrive, hive, jive, contrive, alive, strive, arrive, live
ix	fix, mix, six
oad	road, goad, load, toad
oar	oar, boar, roar, soar
oast	toast, boast, coast, roast
oat	oat, gloat, boat, bloat, throat, float, coat, moat, goat, stoat
ob	fob, mob, blob, job, cob, slob, sob, gob, snob, Bob, knob, rob, lob
ock	mock, sock, block, jock, smock, stock, shock, clock, knock, dock, lock, pock, rock, frock, cock, crock, flock, hock, o'clock
od	cod, sod, god, plod, nod, pod, shod, prod, clod, rod
ode	ode, strode, code, lode, mode, rode
odge	dodge, lodge
off	off, toff, doff
oft	loft, soft
og	log, bog, jog, clog, smog, slog, hog, fog, cog, dog, frog
oil	oil, soil, broil, coil, boil, toilet, spoil, foil, toil
oin	coin, join, loin
oke	coke, stoke, joke, smoke, poke, woke, awoke, stroke, broke, spoke, bloke, choke, yoke
old	old, hold, bold, sold, cold, fold, scold, told, mold, gold
ole	hole, whole, mole, role, sole, stole
oll	doll, scroll, loll, poll, roll, troll, toll
ome	home, dome
on	con, don, yon
ond	bond, fond, pond, frond, blond
one	alone, bone, clone, cone, drone, hone, lone, phone, prone, stone, throne, tone
ong	long, strong, bong, along, song, thong, throng, prong
onk	honk, clonk

Rhymes	
oo	boo, coo, goo, woo, moo, shoo, zoo, igloo, too
ood	mood, food, brood
ood	good, stood, hood, wood
oof	proof, hoof, aloof, goof, spoof, roof
ook	book, cook, chook, hook, look, nook, brook, crook, rook, shook, took
ool	stool, pool, school, fool, cool, spool, tool, drool
oom	boom, broom, bloom, loom, groom, gloom, doom, room, zoom
oon	spoon, moon, boon, balloon, noon, loon, croon, soon, goon, swoon
oop	hoop, stoop, coop, scoop, swoop, snoop, droop, loop, troop
oor	poor, door, moor, floor, spoor
oot	foot, soot
oot*	boot, scoot, hoot, loot, root, shoot, toot
op	crop, bop, pop, cop, top, hop, lop, flop, clop, sop, slop, mop, plop, drop, prop, stop, chop, shop
ope	rope, scope, cope, grope, dope, mope, slope, pope
or	ambassador, doctor, error, actor, conductor, ancestor, author, radiator, editor, contractor, visitor, traitor, bachelor, collector, competitor, conqueror, inventor, professor, successor, governor, survivor, inspector, instructor
ore	store, sore, bore, wore, core, tore, spore, snore, pore, lore, fore, shore, gore, swore, chore, before, restore, more, ore, score, yore
ork	cork, fork, pork, stork
orn	born, thorn, corn, adorn, horn, shorn, forlorn, worn, morn, scorn, torn
ort	fort, short, port, sort, sport, abort, snort
osh	posh, gosh, slosh
oss	moss, gloss, toss, loss, doss, floss
ost	cost, lost, frost
ot	cot, dot, got, clot, blot, plot, spot, jot, apricot, forgot, knot, squat, trot, hot, slot, tot, not, lot, pot, rot, bot, shot
otch	botch, notch, blotch, utch
ote	note, dote, tote
ouble	double, trouble
oud	loud, cloud, proud
ough	rough, tough, enough
ough	cough, trough
ought	fraught, wrought, bought, fought, naught, caught, aught, brought, distraught, taught, ought, sought, thought
ould	could, would, should

Rhymes	
ounce	ounce, bounce, pounce, trounce, flounce
ound	hound, bound, round, mound, crowned, around, ground, pound, found, surround, sound, wound
ount	count, mount, account
oup	soup, group
our	our, hour, sour, flour
ouse	grouse, mouse, louse, spouse, house, douse
out	stout, out, tout, bout, flout, lout, pout, trout, grout, clout, spout, rout, snout, shout, about, gout, sprout, scout
ove	wove, grove, cove, rove, clove, stove, drove
ove	dove, love, glove, shove, above
ow	bow, crow, ago, although, below, blow, dough, flow, glow, go, grow, hoe, know, low, mow, row, sew, show, slow, snow, sow, stow, though, throw, toe, tow
ow	now, bow, cow, chow, brow, how, plow, sow, vow, wow
owl	owl, howl, prowl, growl, scowl
own	own, sown, blown, grown, thrown
own	drown, crown, clown, down, brown, frown, gown, nightgown, town
ox	box, fox, cox
oy	boy, cloy, coy, annoy, joy, toy, destroy, enjoy, ploy
oze	froze, bows, hose, nose, rose, toes, those, grows, flows, doze, blows, prose, pose, chose, close
ub	snub, dub, club, pub, grub, drub, nub, stub, scrub, cub, rub, sub, shrub, tub, hub
ube	cube, tube
uch	much, such, hutch, clutch, crutch
uck	shuck, buck, duck, pluck, luck, stuck, truck, suck, yuck, cluck, muck, puck, struck, chuck, tuck
ud	bud, dud, cud, mud, thud
udge	judge, nudge, fudge, sludge, smudge, grudge, budge
ue	cue, clue, due, hue, rue, value, flue, blue, glue
uff	bluff, cuff, fluff, muff, huff, puff, ruff, snuff, stuff, gruff, scruff, chuff
ug	shrug, glug, smug, mug, bug, drug, snug, slug, chug, pug, dug, tug, plug, jug, thug, hug, rug, lug
ull	full, pull, bull
ull	cull, mull, dull, skull, gull, hull, scull, lull
um	scrum, bum, sum, glum, Mum, drum, chum, swum, rum, strum, gum, yum, plum, hum, slum
ump	bump, plump, clump, lump, trump, slump, chump, pump, thump, dump, grump, rump, hump, jump, stump

Rhymes	
un	nun, bun, fun, gun, one, outdone, shun, spun, won, son, ton, ton, none, undone, pun, run, sun, stun, begun, done
unch	bunch, lunch, punch, crunch
une	June, tune
ung	sprung, bung, rung, dung, clung, sung, hung, stung, flung, slung, swung, lung, strung
unk	trunk, dunk, punk, bunk, clunk, sunk, hunk, skunk, flunk, plunk, drunk, junk, chunk, shrunk, stunk
unt	bunt, stunt, hunt, punt, runt, blunt
up	cup, pup, sup
urn	urn, burn, turn, churn, spurn
urt	curt, hurt, spurt
us	pus, plus
use	use, refuse, fuse, muse, amuse, abuse
ush	hush, plush, lush, brush, mush, rush, crush, flush, blush
usk	dusk, husk, tusk
ust	bust, crust, dust, thrust, gust, must, trust, rust
ut	cut, nut, glut, gut, jut, but, hut, rut, mutt, putt, shut
ute	cute, brute, jute, lute, mute, flute
y	why, by, ply, pry, dry, fry, spy, shy, cry, sky, fly, try, my

Syllables

Prefix/Root/Suffix Identify and remove affixes	art•ist, ask•ing, be•side, big•ger, book•let, boss•y, care•ful, climb•ing, clos•est, com•ing, cook•ing, dark•ness, small•er, deep•er, dis•cover, dream•ing, drown•ing, farm•er, fore•cast, friend•ly, hot•ter, salt•y, itch•y, loud•er, luck•y, sleep•y, mis•take, morn•ing, pack•age, pain•less, pay•ment, peace•ful, plant•ed, quick•ly, re•pay, slow•est, soft•ly, stop•ping, sweet•er, tall•est, think•ing, thirst•y, throw•ing, treat•ment, un•fair, want•ed, warm•est, wind•y
VC/CV Divide between consonants	af•ter bal•loon, ber•ry, blis•ter, cot•ton, bot•tle, but•ter, but•ton, cab•bage, can•dle, car•rot, cir•cle, cof•fee, com•mon, con•tract, coun•cil, let•ter, cus•tom, diz•zy, en•joy, bas•ket, fol•low, ap•ple, fun•ny, hel•lo, hur•ry, lad•der, let•tuce, mat•tress, mon•key, of•fice, den•tist, pen•cil, pic•nic, pic•ture, plas•tic, plen•ty, prob•lem, cur•rent, fif•teen, pump•kin, hel•met, pur•ple, rab•bit, for•get, rib•bon, el•bow, pup•py, scis•sors, hap•pen, sen•tence, sil•ly, sis•ter, kit•ten, soc•cer, sub•ject, sum•mer, thun•der, whis•per, win•dow, win•ter
VC/V	mon•ey, ol•ive, pan•ic, ped•al, pit•y, pres•ent, rad•ish, rap•id, riv•er, sal•ad, sev•en, shov•el, stud•y, top•ic, trav•el, vis•it, vol•ume, wid•ow, bod•y, buck•et, cit•y, clev•er, clin•ic, cop•y, fin•ish, for•est, hon•ey, lem•on, lev•el, lim•it, liz•ard, men•u, met•al
V/CV	ba•by, ba•con, ba•sic, be•hind, de•stroy, do•nate, e•qual, e•ven, fe•ver, fi•nal, fla•vor, ho•tel, la•bel, la•dy, le•gal, mi•nus, mo•ment, mu•sic, na•tion, o•pen, o•val, pa•per, pho•to, pi•lot, po•ny, pre•tend, pri•vate, ra•zor, rea•son, re•cess, se•cret, si•lent, spi•der, ta•ble, ti•dy, ti•ger, to•tal, tu•na, va•cant, vi•rus, ze•ro
Syllables - Longer Words	a•gree•ment, ac•ci•den•tal, ar•range•ment, bak•er•y, but•ter•fly, cel•e•bra•tion, cit•i•zen•ship, com•fort•a•ble, cat•er•pil•lar, com•pe•ti•tion, com•pli•cat•ed, com•put•er, coun•sel•or, cu•cum•ber, cus•tom•er, de•liv•er•y, dem•o•crat•ic, di•ag•no•sis, dis•a•gree•ment, dis•lo•cat•ed, doc•u•ment, em•bar•rass•ing, en•er•gy, en•gage•ment, es•sen•tial, fash•ion•a•ble, fav•or•ite, fi•nan•cial, fu•ner•al, gov•ern•ment, graf•fi•ti, guar•an•tee, hel•i•cop•ter, in•di•vid•u•al, in•fec•tion, in•no•cent, in•tel•li•gent, in•tro•duc•tion, kin•der•gar•ten, mi•gra•tion, me•di•um, med•i•ca•tion, mes•sen•ger, mis•be•hav•ior, mos•qui•to, re•mem•ber, sig•na•ture, won•der•ful

Split digraph minimal pairs

This is not intended as a complete list of split digraphs but is a list of minimal pairs with split digraphs. It can be useful to do exercises with familiar words, such as *tap* and *tape*, to help learners identify the differences in sounds.

a	a_e	e	e_e	i	i_e	o	o_e	u	u_e
Al	ale	her	here	bit	bite	cod	code	cub	cube
at	ate	pet	Pete	fill	file	con	cone	cut	cute
back	bake	till	tile	fin	fine	cop	cope	duck	duke
Cam	came	Tim	time	grip	gripe	doll	dole	quack	quake
can	cane			hid	hide	hop	hope	quit	quite
cap	cape			kit	kite	not	note	tub	tube
car	care			lick	like	pop	pope		
far	fare			mill	mile	rob	robe		
fat	fate			pill	pile	rod	rode		
hat	hate			pin	pine	slop	slope		
Jan	Jane			pip	pipe				
mad	made			rid	ride				
man	mane			rip	ripe				
mat	mate			shin	shine				
pan	pane			Sid	side				
past	paste			sit	site				
plan	plane			slid	slide				
rack	rake			slim	slime				
rat	rate			spin	spine				
Sal	sale			strip	stripe				
scar	scare			trip	tripe				
scrap	scrape			twin	twine				
star	stare			win	wine				
tap	tape			snip	snipe				
van	vane								
rag	rage								
slat	slate								

Word chains

fat, sat, mat, map, nap, lap, lad, bad, bat, rat, hat, ham, jam, ram, rag, ran, tan, tab, tap, tag, wag, bag, ban, van, fan
win, pin, pit, bit, lit, sit, hit, him, jim, tim, tip, zip, lip, lid, kid, bid, big, wig, fig, fin, tin
hot, hog, dog, dot, rot, rob, sob, sod, pod, pot, hot, hop, top
mug, mud, bud, bus, bun, run, rub, tub, tug, rug, hug, hum, hut, nut, but, rut, rum, yum
bit, bat, sat, sit, fit, fat, fan, fin, win, tin, tan, tap, lap, lip, hip, hit, hat, ham, him
fan, fin, pin, pit, pot, pat, pan, pad, bad, lad, lid, rid, rod, nod, not, hot, hat, hit
ran, run, fun, bun, bud, bid, bad, had, hid, lid, lad, sad, sag, bag, big, bug, hug, hum
fat, fit, sit, sat, set, wet, bet, bit, big, bug, mug, mud, mad, man, men, ten, tin, fin, fun
fig, rig, rug, bug, bun, fun, fin, fit, hit, hat
mat, map, lap, lip, tip, top, tot, got, get, wet, net, not, nut
fast, cast, last, list, lint, lent, sent, send, sand, band, bend, bent, best, vest, vent, rent, rant, raft
last, lost, loft, left, lept, lent, lint, lift, list, lisp, wisp, wimp, limp, lump, lamp, ramp
felt, belt, best, west, wept, welt, pelt, pest, rest, rust, dust, must, must, mist, mint, mink, sink, sank, sunk, dunk, hunk, hunt, punt, punk, junk
mask, task, tank, sank, sand, send, bend, bent, belt, welt, weld, held, meld, mend, tend, tent, sent
slap, slop, slip, slit, spit, spot, slot, slat, flat, flap, flip, clip, clop, crop, drop, drip, trip, trim, grim, gram, grab, crab, crib
flat, slat, slap, slip, flip, flop, slop, stop, step, stem, stim, slim, skim, skin, spin, spun, spud, sped, sled, bled, fled, Fred
flab, blab, blob, blot, clot, clop, flop, flip, slip, slim, slam, slap, flap, clap
crash, trash, trap, rap, chap, chip, ship, sip, rip, rich, rib, rub, chub, chum, chump, thump, lump, limp, chimp, champ, lamp, ramp, cramp, cram, crash
rash, thrash, thrush, brush, blush, plush, flush, flash, lash, sash, mash, mush, shush, shut, hut, hat, that, chat, rat, rut, rush, crush
math, mash, sash, dash, dish, fish, wish, swish, swim, slim, slum, slam, slash, clash, lash, lush, mush, mud, thud, thug, chug, bug, bag, bath
stump, stamp, scamp, camp, lamp, lump, clump, clamp, clasp, claps, flaps, laps, lap, lip
crunch, brunch, branch, brand, bland, land, sand, stand, strand
strap, strip, strips, trips, rips, lips, clips
trip, trap, tramp, trump, crump, clump, plump, slump, stump,
split, splat, slat, slant, scant, scan, scam, scram, scrap, scraps

Further reading and resources

Instructor resources

Letters and Sounds: Principles and Practice of High Quality Phonics

This program from the UK is designed for young children, but it could be adapted.

https://www.gov.uk/government/uploads/system/uploads/attach ment_data/file/190599/Letters_and_Sounds_-_DFES-00281-2007.pdf

MiniLit and MultiLit
MULTILIT (Making up lost time in literacy). Revised ed.

Macquarie University. Special Education Centre

Macquarie University Special Education Centre, Sydney, 2007

http://www.multilit.com/

These are excellent catch-up programs that have been designed to be used in schools, but aspects of the training and program potentially could be adapted to an adult context.

MUSEC Briefings
Macquarie University Special Education Centre - community-outreach

This website gives short, accessible reviews of education intervention strategies. The reviews give short summaries of the rationale behind teaching approaches and clear statements regarding whether an approach is supported by evidence or not. Although the site is primarily focussed on special education, some sections may be relevant for early literacy instruction of adults.

Oz Mnemonics: Memory Aids for Spelling Irregularly Spelt Words (for Teachers and Parents)

Alison Rowe

Focus Educational Resources, 1997

These mnemonics may be useful for learners, or they may simply be a useful template for developing relevant memory tools for learners.

The Phonics Handbook

Sue Lloyd and Sara Wernham

Jolly Learning, Chigwell, 2013

Jolly Phonics is a well-structured phonics program but inappropriate for adult learners because the images and vocabulary have been designed for young children. The resources may be useful for instructors to adapt to the needs of their classes.

Tree or Three? An Elementary Pronunciation Course

Ann Baker

Cambridge University Press, Cambridge, 2006

Ship or Sheep? An Intermediate Pronunciation Course

Ann Baker

Cambridge University Press, Cambridge, 2006

These are staples of English language teaching classrooms and have been for a long time. In ESL classrooms, the books are usually used in the development of pronunciation skills, but the material can be used in phonemic awareness exercises.

Words Their Way

Pearson Education Limited

This is a series of books in a spelling program. The resources are not appropriate for beginners, but it may be a useful series of resources for people who have an advanced vocabulary and are more proficient at reading.

Handwriting and formatting

Dyslexia Style Guide
This is a clear style guide from the British Dyslexia Association about meeting the needs of learners with dyslexia.
http://www.bdadyslexia.org.uk/common/ckeditor/filemanager/userfiles/About_Us/policies/Dyslexia_Style_Guide.pdf

KG Primary Penmanship
This is a useful font for creating handwriting practice worksheets that are targeted to the specific needs of learners, although there are others. It is currently available for free download from a few sites.

Language Resources

Phoneme inventory
http://phoible.org/
This is a useful inventory of the sounds in some languages; it can help instructors if they know which sounds learners are most likely to struggle with because they are not present in their languages of origin. The interface is not particularly easy to use, but it is worth exploring the site.

World Atlas of Language Structures (WALS)
http://wals.info/
This is a large database of structural properties of languages. It is not a teaching resource but may help make informed decisions about the sequence to introduce sounds and the areas in which learners are likely to need additional support.

Glossary

Automaticity: Reading becomes a process that does not require deliberate decoding of each word; it involves quick, accurate recognition of words. A learner who has developed automaticity might still read a text like it is a list of words rather than a story; automaticity is a component of reading, but it is not the only skill that is required.

Blending: the process of putting sounds together to make a word. /r e d/ gets blended together to make the word *red*. This is one of the key skills in reading.

Cognitive load: The amount of mental effort used by the working memory.

Continuant: A sound, such as /f s th/, that can be sustained.

CVC words: Consonant-vowel-consonant words, such as *sit*, and *hat*. *Pink* is CVCC and *blink* is CCVCC. This relates to sounds rather than letters; *rain* is CVC and *black* is CCVC.

Decodable: Sounds and spelling patterns that the learner has already studied. Words that are, or are not, decodable will depend on the reading skills of the learner. Once the letters *u* and *t*, and the *sh* digraph have been introduced to a class, the word *shut* is decodable.

Digraph: Two letters representing one sound, such as *ch*, *th*, and *ea*.

Exonym: Name for a place people or language that is used outside that region or language. For example, *Germany* is the name of a country that is used in English, and *Deutschland* is the name that is used within the country. *Deutsch* is the name of the language, and *Deutsche* is used to refer to the people, while outside of the country, the language is called *German*, the same as the term for the nationality.

For people learning English in Australia, exonyms of their country of origin and the languages spoken are essential vocabulary because terms like *Putonghua* (Mandarin), or *Druk Yul* (Bhutan) are less likely to be recognised in official contexts. It may also be worth reiterating the names *Australia* and *English*, given that these also have exonyms (for example, the English language is referred to as *yīngyǔ* in Mandarin, and *Inggılızchä* in Uyghur).

Fluency: Being able to read texts in meaningful chunks, with pauses in appropriate places. Fluency is context specific; someone who is a confident reader may not read fluently if the topic is outside their knowledge or experience, such as reading a set of AFL rules or a medical textbook.

Letter blends: Combinations of two or more letters in a word. Both sounds can be heard, such as the *gr* in *green*, the *st* in *stop*, or the *rt* in *short*. It is much more effective to teach the process of blending than to teach specific letter blends.

Onset: The initial consonant or consonant blend in a word before a vowel. *Str* in *strong*, or *b* in *big*. Some words such as *each*, do not have an onset.

Oral blending: The process of hearing sounds and putting them together to make a word. *b i g* makes the word *big*. This skill is needed before people can blend letters written on a page.

Orthographic rules: The sets of conventions about how words are written. There are multiple ways to write most sounds in English, and orthographic rules are the guidelines as to which representation is applied in a given word.

Phoneme: The smallest chunks of sound in words. The word *bend* has four phonemes /b e n d/, and the word *broom* has four as well /b r oo m/.

Phonemic awareness: The understanding that words are made up of sounds and being able to manipulate those sounds. It is a very strong predictor of future reading skills.

Position, final: The final sound in a word, such as the /g/ in *big* and the /t/ in *right*.

Position, initial: The first sound in a word, such as the /b/ in *big* and the /r/ in *right*.

Position, medial: The middle sound in a word, such as the /i/ in *big* and the /igh/ in *right*.

Prestige variety: It is possible that learners fluently speak a variant form of English, such as learners from Liberia or Bangladesh. These languages and dialects are just as effective for declarations of love, telling fibs, telling jokes, and teasing siblings as any other language or dialect, which is what languages are for; communicating with the people around us. As effective as languages and dialects are, other dialects of English are not given much status in Australia, and outside linguistic circles (where people may be rubbing their hands together with glee at encountering such an interesting dialect), would generally be regarded as 'incorrect'. The standard accent and structure used in Australia has much more status as a language than other dialects of English, such as Singaporean English. It is worth using the term 'Australian English' rather than 'correct English'; learners may have grown up speaking a dialect with family and friends, possibly hearing the dialect on local television and movies, and being told that a language that they have spoken all their life is 'wrong' is not going to be helpful.

Realia: Objects from real life that are used in the classroom, such as different sized bottles when teaching language related to volume and measurement. Realia tends to be a very useful tool in language classrooms.

Rime: The vowel and final part of a word or syllable. *Ong* in *strong*, or *ig* in *big*.

Root: Part of a word. For example, *bio*, meaning life, is the root word in *biodegradable, biography, biology, biosphere, microbiology, symbiotic*.

Schwa: A neutral, unstressed vowel sound. /ə/, such as in *about, the, sister*.

Segmenting: Breaking words up into the component sounds. The word *went* has the sounds /w e n t/.

Stop: The sounds /p t k b g d/. Sounds that are made by stopping the flow of air. They cannot be extended without changing the sound.

Synthetic phonics: An approach to teaching reading that starts with the link between sounds in words and the way that those sounds are represented by letters on a page. Sounds are synthesised together.

Printed in Great Britain
by Amazon

60770532R00093